GREAT CENTRAL RAILWAY

MAIN LINE OPERATIONS AROUND

MANCHESTER AND THE MSW ELECTRIFICATION

ALBERT WOOD,
PEAK FOREST WHARF, DUCIE STREET,
LONDON ROAD, MANCHESTER.

Daily Express Service of Boats

National Telephone: 4934 MANCHESTER.

TO AND FROM

MANCHESTER, ASHTON, HYDE, MARPLE, STRINES, NEW MILLS, BUGSWORTH, & WHALEY BRIDGE;

Also BOLLINGTON, MACCLESFIELD, etc., etc.

Goods received at Peak Forest Wharf, Ducie Street, London Road, Manchester, up to 6 p.m. (2 p.m. on

Above left: **Poster, no date.** For over forty years, the canals in the Manchester area had a real monopoly on transporting bulky goods, until they were eclipsed by the railways. The two modes of transport had an intimate relationship, the railway following the canals. A canal map is almost as congested as that of railways, with connections right through the centre linking to the Bridgewater canal as well as the rivers in the west too. The MS&LR bought out the competition of the Ashton, Peak Forest and Macclesfield Canals in 1846. Many still continued to have a different role to play and this bill, illustrating the places served, was almost mirrored subsequently by the railways. Later, the development of the Ship Canal brought a new source of goods, to be transported inland by railways. (Courtesy of Manchester Libraries, Information & Archives, Manchester City Council m53789)

Top right: **Guide Bridge, around 1920.** Heading west past the goods depot and about to enter the station is O5 class No 412, built just up the line at Gorton in 1917. These Robinson designed engines were there the mainstay of the company's goods hauling fleet. Upon entering the locomotive repair shop in 1922, it was rebuilt to class O4, witness the individual splasher for the first pair of driving wheels and, had a '5' added as a prefix to its number. It survived until 1965. (Real Photographs)

Right: **Manchester Central, 1949.** The famous Liverpool to Harwich Boat Train starts from Manchester Central behind B1 class 4-6-0 No 61150. While not 'pure' GCR territory, the company was joint partners with the GN and MR railway in the Cheshire Lines Railway. Soon the train will speed through the suburbs of Manchester where it will run onto its own company's lines. At Fallowfield, it will meet the main line from London Road and continue east towards Sheffield. (E Oldham Coltas Trust)

Cover pictures.
Front: Celebrated locomotive, A3 Pacific No 60103 *Flying Scotsman* waits at platform 'A' at London Road station with an express for the capital. (Eric Oldham, Coltas Trust)

Rear, top: **London Road roof, 2016.** This set of twin pillars mark the original shed, to the right, and the 1866 extension on the left. The latter became the haunt of the L&NWR while the tenant (the 'Sheffield Company') occupied the shed on the right. (BPC)

Rear, bottom: **New electric train.** To celebrate the opening of the electric line from Manchester to Sheffield, a series of 'artist' impression' cards were published. Here an EM1 class, in green livery, using just one pantograph hauls a mixed freight train. (Commercial Postcard)

GREAT CENTRAL RAILWAY

MAIN LINE OPERATIONS AROUND
MANCHESTER AND THE MSW ELECTRIFICATION

BOB PIXTON

PEN & SWORD
TRANSPORT
AN IMPRINT OF PEN & SWORD BOOKS LTD.
YORKSHIRE – PHILADELPHIA

First published in Great Britain in 2020 by
Pen and Sword Transport
An imprint of
Pen & Sword Books Ltd
Yorkshire - Philadelphia

ISBN 978 1 52673 591 1

Typeset in Palatino 11/13 by Aura Technology and Software Services, India.

Printed and bound in India by Replika Press Pvt. Ltd.

Pen & Sword Books Ltd incorporates the Imprints of Pen & Sword Books Archaeology, Atlas, Aviation, Battleground, Discovery, Family History, History, Maritime, Military, Naval, Politics, Railways, Select, Transport, True Crime, Fiction, Frontline Books, Leo Cooper, Praetorian Press, Seaforth Publishing, Wharncliffe and White Owl.

For a complete list of Pen & Sword titles please contact

PEN & SWORD BOOKS LIMITED
47 Church Street, Barnsley, South Yorkshire, S70 2AS, England
E-mail: enquiries@pen-and-sword.co.uk
Website: www.pen-and-sword.co.uk

or

PEN AND SWORD BOOKS
1950 Lawrence Rd, Havertown, PA 19083, USA
E-mail: Uspen-and-sword@casematepublishers.com
Website: www.penandswordbooks.com

CONTENTS

INTRODUCTION TO THE GREAT CENTRAL SERIES

The York Hotel in Manchester has an important place in the history of this line through the Pennines. It was the place where investors decided to back, and then sack, the idea of a line to Sheffield. At that time, the early 1830s, it took goods over a week, in fine weather, by a circuitous canal system, or two days, in good weather, by horse and cart, to pass between the two towns. Businesses all over the country were crying out for better communications.

The opening of the railway between Liverpool and Manchester on 15 September 1830 had so exceeded its promoters' expectations that many other towns wanted this latest venture and a share in the profits it could bring. Speculators had been very successful with their investments in canals, many seeing a return of 50 per cent each

York Hotel, 1849.
(Crown Copyright)

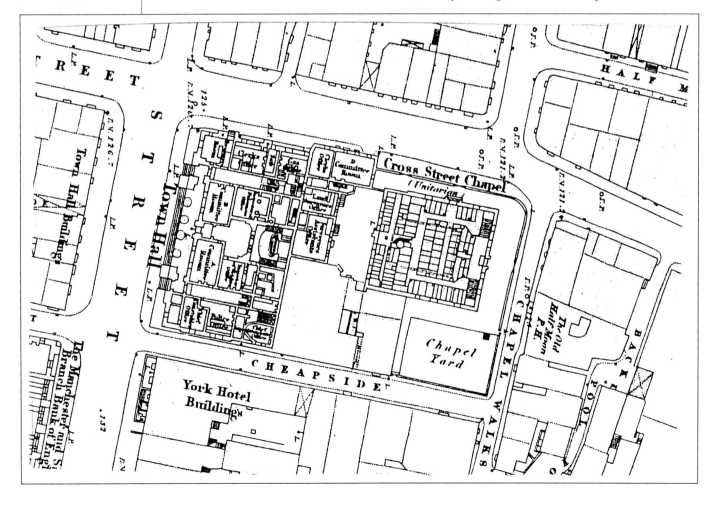

Seal of Sheffield & Manchester Railway (twice actual size).

year. Consequently, subsequent railway schemes were seen in a similar light: a licence to print money.

On 20 October 1831, a group of like-minded businessmen met here to formulate a Sheffield and Manchester Railway. However, unlike the relatively flat terrain across Lancashire, there was the question of the Pennines to overcome. While the Rainhill Trials had meant that trains could be hauled up and down the incline planes between Liverpool and Manchester, the Pennines presented an altogether different proposition.

Less than two years later, on 5 June 1833, a meeting of the Board of Directors heard that there were two fundamental objections to the plans. They were undecided about two key matters: how to penetrate the Pennines; and the use of incline planes where stationary engines would pull wagons up. There was also disagreement about if they should pass along the Hope or Don river valleys on the approach to Sheffield. Consequently, they agreed to abandon completely the Sheffield & Manchester Railway, returning the balance of money to investors. An irony of the situation that subsequently unfolded is that now the route between the two cities is through Stockport, via the Goyt gap at New Mills, penetrating the Pennines and then passing along the Hope Valley towards Sheffield, much the same as one of the original proposals!

Surprisingly, in this time of massive investment and profits, nothing happened for almost three years. In the background were canals with investors wanting profit today rather than modest returns tomorrow. It wasn't until the winter of 1836 that meetings were held at Sheffield in the Cutler's Hall on 4 January; Manchester in the York Hotel, 5 January; and Stalybridge at the Eagle Inn, on 19 February.

There, businessmen resolved to build a line between the two towns again. However, this time it would pass through Ashton under Lyne, and have branches to Stalybridge and Glossop too. The valleys of rivers flowing from the Pennines were to be utilised, Etherow (to the west) and Don (to the east). This received its Royal Assent on 5 May 1837.

The first formal meeting of the Directors of the Sheffield, Ashton under Lyne and Manchester Railway met at Penistone (probably at the Rose & Crown Inn), on 3 November 1837 to oversee the project to link the towns in the title.

There was plenty of optimism in this new venture. Technology had moved on with the development of new engines. So, with a three-mile tunnel through the Pennines and gradients no greater than 1 in 120, the promoters hoped to overcome the disadvantages of the earlier plans. As an attraction to investors, it was proposed

Above left: Plaque, 2013.

Above right: Seal of S&MR.

Cutler's Hall, 2012. There has been a Hall on this site since 1638. This one, the third, dates from 1832, atmospheric pollution has taken the shine from the stone. (BPC)

Eagle Inn, around 1950s. (Courtesy Tameside Library Archive)

Rose & Crown Inn, 2012. Due to the poor trading conditions at the time, in 2010 it ceased to be an inn and became home to a firm of solicitors. (BPC)

that the Manchester end should be in a terminus jointly with the Manchester & Birmingham Railway, and indeed, the 'Sheffield' line was to share tracks for the last ¾ of a mile into the London Road station. At the eastern end, the terminus was to be in a vacant plot of land to the east of the cattle market in central Sheffield.

To reduce expenditure, the Board of Directors decided in August 1838 that the Woodhead tunnel was to be pared down to just a single bore, the Stalybridge branch abandoned and, temporarily, the Sheffield terminus to be brought east to Bridgehouses, which obviated a crossing of the River Don.

Two other ideas were floated around that time. The Chief Engineer, Joseph Locke, suggested that an extension of the line eastwards would enable Sheffield merchants access to the coast and customers in Europe. Also suggested was the idea that at the Manchester end, the line from the terminus should continue on a viaduct to connect to the Liverpool & Manchester Railway in Liverpool Road. This latter project was rejected as it was deemed that the 'time was not mature for such a project'.

Having attracted sufficient support, the first sod was cut near to the western end of the Woodhead tunnel on 1 October 1838 and the first trains ran from Manchester, the most profitable section, on 17 November 1841 to Godley. Under four years later and the Sheffield section opened (14 July 1845), with the whole line being opened just before Christmas (23 December) 1845. On the same date, the line to Stalybridge opened too.

Coat of arms of the SA&M.

Seal of SAMR.

Typical of the times, the newly opened railway sought to lease itself with others, chiefly the Midland and the Manchester & Birmingham Railways. They declined and so amalgamation with both Sheffield & Lincolnshire Junction Railway as well as the Great Grimsby & Sheffield Junction Railway meant a continuous line from Manchester to a port on the east coast.

The Sheffield Ashton under Lyne & Sheffield Railway had its last meeting on 30 December 1846, at the company's offices at Store Street in Manchester, enabling a new company to meet a week later, on 6 January 1847 as the Manchester, Sheffield & Lincolnshire Railway.

Almost fifty years later, with the imminent opening of the London extension the Board discussed how inappropriate the company title now was at a meeting on 27 March 1896. They discussed 'Central' and 'Great Central' with interested parties over subsequent meetings before settling on 'Great Central Railway' from 1 August 1897.

The meeting of Directors on 15 December 1922 was to be the company's last; from the new year, they would be amalgamated with other companies to form the London & North Eastern Railway and twenty five years later, to form British Railways.

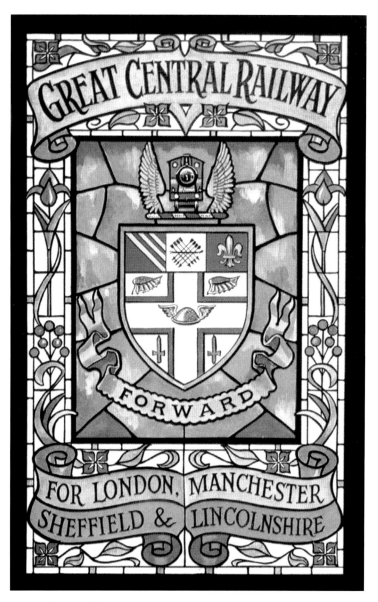

Coat of arms of GCR.

PREFACE

When I set out to consider the feasibility of writing an illustrated history of the company, I had some conditions I wanted to adhere to, one of which was that there would only be pictures of steam engines and another was that the territory investigated would be that in the title of the progenitor; Manchester, Sheffield & Lincolnshire Railway. Although the company was party to the Cheshire Lines Railway and so should be excluded as a 'joint line', to do justice to that railway, however, its size and extent mean that it, apart from minor sections to tell this story, is best left to a further volume of its own.

The time-period would be pre-electrification, wherever possible. The interest in the DC electrics has made me change my criteria a fraction so there is a section, in my view, as to how the line was different since electrification. Apart from that concession, I feel that I have been able to stick to the guiding principles.

This volume concerns itself with the section of the main line at opening, to Godley and the line to Stalybridge. Not long after the opening of the 2nd Manchester Central station and an access link from Fairfield to Chorlton Junction (Manchester Central Station Line) was opened throughout on 2 May 1892. Rather than stopping the account along this line where MS&LR territory ceased and as the traffic along this line emanated

This shows the extent of the company in 1922, prior to the Grouping.

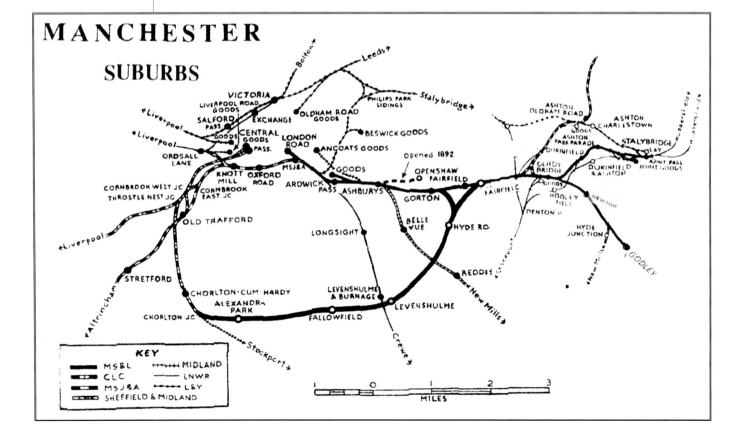

from ventures to the east of Manchester, I have continued the account into Central station, an association with the GNR and the MR in the Cheshire Lines Railway.

The MS&LR engaged in several joint ventures in the area, details of which will be in a later volume. The busy commuter route to Altrincham was such a venture, with the L&NWR opened in 1849 connecting with lines to Chester and Ordsall Lane. Another such undertaking, with the same partner, was to try to break the stranglehold the companies thought the L&Y had on traffic to Oldham. The Oldham, Ashton & Guide Bridge Railway opened in 1861, connecting with the already opened L&NWR link from Oldham to Greenfield on their main line to Yorkshire. The company also joined with the MR to allow the latter company access to Manchester, a town the L&NWR regarded as its territory. They joined to build lines from Hyde (junction) to New Mills (completely by 1865), Ashburys to Romiley (1875) and a branch to Hayfield (1868) were products of co-operation. A link from Marple in 1869, jointly with the North Staffordshire Railway, enable this company access to Manchester. By means of such undertakings the company avoided isolation and brought in extra revenue too.

Manchester Central Good Depot. Whilst most peoples' heads are turned by flashy express engines, it was humble engines, such as this, that the company relied upon. Built by the Manchester, Sheffield and Lincolnshire Railway in 1871, it was class 18A, number 61. Over twenty years later it was re-numbered as No 53 and ten years later still, it was converted to a saddle tank. Testimony to its durability is that it lasted well into LNER days, not being withdrawn until 1929. It is probably on dispay in the goods yard. Conditions on the footplate must have been difficult during inclement weather. (BPC)

THE MAIN LINE TO GODLEY

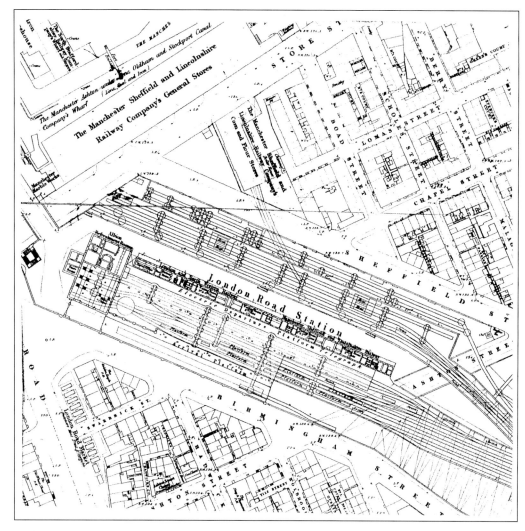

Store Street station, around 1849. The Sheffield Ashton-under-Lyne & Manchester Railway were always tenants to the landlord – the Manchester & Birmingham Railway – at their terminus in Manchester. In fact, they had to pay a toll from the junction of the two lines at Ardwick Junction, the last 1,000yd into the terminal station. Thus, when trains first set out for the east, it wasn't along their own metals, neither was it from London Road, as this wasn't finished. Instead they set off on 17 November 1841 from a temporary station, probably of wooden construction, in Travis Street, a few hundred yards short of Store Street. The landlord had been running trains to the south for the past eighteen months, since 4 June in the previous year. When Store Street eventually was opened, on 10 May 1842, there were just two platforms which the two companies shared, one for arrivals and one for departures. As was typical of the thinking in railway circles of the day, the two platforms were separated by tracks (four in this case) all connected by small turntables which were used to store wagons. Passengers wanting to depart from the station would enter the building through doorways on the right where the two railway companies had separate booking offices and waiting rooms. Ideal as this sounds, the 'Sheffield' company had to share facilities until 2 June, a year after the permanent station opened, illustrating tensions between landlord and tenant. As well as the 'official' title of London Road, to many it was 'Bank Top' station, the whole structure being on viaduct some forty feet above the road level. Note the Albion Refreshment Rooms at the left-hand end of the station and the set of steps beyond, leading down to street level. (Crown Copyright: Godfrey Edition)

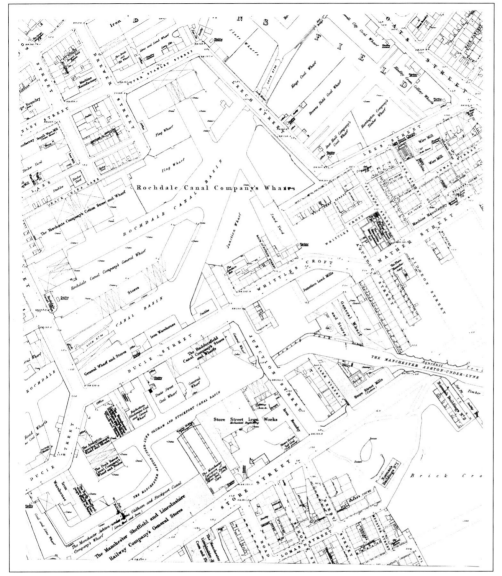

***Above*: Piccadilly, 1849.** Canals had been the dominant movers of goods, usually bulky items, for the past fifty years, that was the competition that the early railway promoters faced, for finances too, their dividends were often massive, 50 per cent annually, was not uncommon. (Crown Copyright: Godfrey Edition)

***Top right*: Store Street aqueduct, 1903.** The Ashton canal, which opened in 1797, connected the coal mines in Ashton under Lyne with customers in Manchester. There are four such structures along the way. The canal was incorporated into the Sheffield, Ashton under Lyne & Manchester Railway, the fore-runner of the Manchester, Sheffield & Lincolnshire Railway, as early as 1846. Also known as Shooters Brook aqueduct, it was the first one to be built at a skew, of 45 degrees, and is now a Grade II listed building. At the other end, it connects by means of an aqueduct to the Peak Forest Canal so enabling limestone to be carried to industries. Here, the canal crosses a road at an angle and this is one of the first examples of a skew bridge construction. It connected to the Rochdale canal here. A junction with the Huddersfield Canal in Ashton permitted goods to be carried through the Pennines from the manufacturing areas of Yorkshire. (Courtesy of Manchester Libraries, Information & Archives, Manchester City Council)

***Right*: Dale Street offices, 1895.** The Rochdale Canal also had wharves, warehouses and offices in this part of the town, opening in 1804. It also had connections with other canal systems over the Pennines so that goods from Yorkshire could arrive here. By its extension through Manchester, this canal connected with the Bridgewater canal and so to the Midlands and Liverpool. Under Whittle's Croft was a short piece of canal connecting the Rochdale and Ashton Canals. (Courtesy of Manchester Libraries, Information & Archives, Manchester City Council m56792)

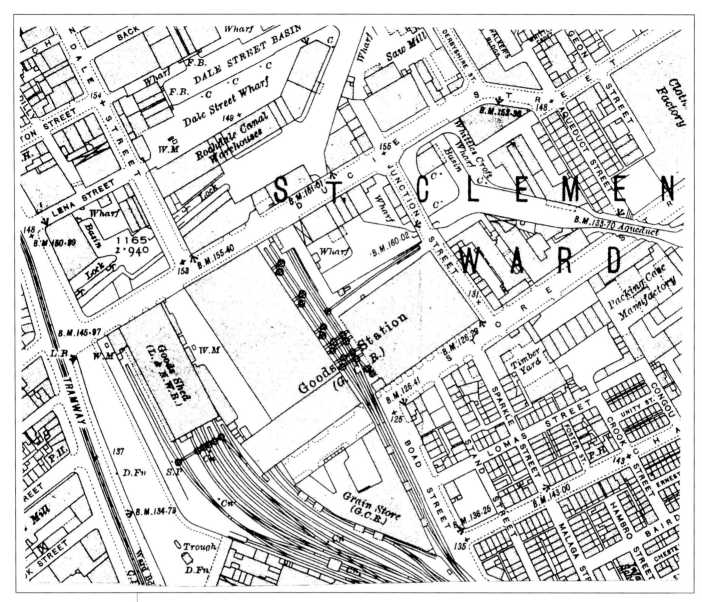

Expansion of London Road goods lines. The early railway promoters underestimated the growth of their lines as they became more successful. Not only was the passenger side of business here increasing meaning the development of extra platforms (which is still continuing today!) but the freight side also enlarged. Having taken over the Ashton canal in 1846, and a lot of its business too, the MS&LR decided to build on its newly acquired premises, right in the middle of the town. Originating with the Act that enlarged the passenger side in 1861, this also gave powers to enlarge facilities here too. Adjacent to lock no 85 on the Rochdale canal, it straightened out Ducie Street, filled in part of the canal and built warehouses. To access them it extended its lines across Sheffield Street.

Opposite below: **Ducie Street, 1953**, viewed from the station buildings' window, shows the rail side of the warehouse. On the right is a low wall, below which is Store Street. The two tracks entering the building are featured on the iron work next to Boad Street. The seven-story building to the rear, is today's luxury apartments, 'The Place', was once the MS&LR's 'London warehouse' being built on land that once belonged to the Ashton canal. The shadow on the right is cast by a five-storey grain warehouse on Store Street.
(Courtesy of Manchester Libraries, Information & Archives, Manchester City Council), BKB Green)

Boad Street, by means of this massive iron viaduct, crossed Store Street to access its new premises. To allow goods to reach the higher levels of its grain store, hoists were built on the outside of the building with wooden covers.

Servicing the goods facilities at London Road

North east of the passenger station were extensive warehouses belonging to the two companies. These were supplied by two, double track approaches, high above Sheffield Street, which ran the length of the passenger station behind the wall of platform A, with a lower, street level set of warehouses.

Above: **GC engine, around 1920.** Of course, to move the wagons, especially fitted freights, high performance engines were needed. Resplendent in its black livery is one of the class 8M 2-8-0s, built in 1918, seen here waiting outside London Road station. Engine No 420 seen here took part in a remarkable scientific experiment which lasted from 1920-4. The 'hump' in the tender is the adaptation to carry pulverised coal (60 per cent) and oil (40 per cent). Rather reminiscent of the trials in 1950s using the ex-Worsborough banker, this engine was tested in its ability to haul 80 empty wagons, and a brake, from Dewsnap sidings to Dunford bridge. Unaltered sister engine No 419 was used as a control engine and their performances compared. Inconclusive test results led their suspension: the lower cost of fuel was largely offset by the costs of its preparation and storage, the company having built a special plant at Gorton to prepare the fuel. (RK Blencowe Negative Archive)

Opposite above: **1948.** Probably whilst acting as station pilot, LNER J11 0-6-0 No 4401, rests between sorting out vans from express trains to and from the goods yard. Not only were the alterations to the couplings hazardous in itself, but the emergence from between wagons into the narrow land between lines was particularly dangerous: hence the men waiting for a suitable opportunity to perform his duties. (BWL Brooksbank)

Ducie Street, pre-Great War. To move wagons into position, the company used engines such as this 0-6-0ST No 279. In their premises between Store and Ducie Streets, there were numerous wagon turntables. With equine assistance, aided by ropes and capstans, wagons were turned and sent into the buildings. (J Quick collection) (TG Wassell, H Davies)

London Road station approach

LONDON ROAD STATION. MANCHESTER.

This page, 1895 left and 1905 right. The next twenty or so years after opening, up to 1866, were turbulent years for the two companies sharing the station. As they both promoted routes to London, the competitive elements were bound to cause friction. However, seeing that they both co-operated in the South Junction line west to Ordsall Lane and Altrincham, then a sharing environment was necessary. Due to growth in the system, both thought that there was more profit in burying the hatchet rather than wielding it. Growth wasn't without chaos though. The Mayor of the Town presided over a public meeting when both Victoria and London Road were described as 'the shabbiest, dingiest and most inadequate and inconvenient that could be found in a town of third or fourth rate importance'. There was gross overcrowding, so much so that passengers had to, 'thread their way through the congregated cans, paddling through intervening pools of milk' and were, 'constantly perplexed, carried off in the wrong train or left behind'. Not surprisingly, the tenant (MS&LR) blamed the landlord (L&NWR) even after they had secured an Act for a new joint station. So, in 1859 the landlord and tenant agreed to partition the station, by the widening of the double track approach and the enlargement of the station. This was cemented by an agreement of 3 October 1861 with both parties agreeing to construct and run a joint passenger station which was to be built and equally divided. While the extension train shed was ready by the December of 1866, the station would have been if not for a serious accident in the January of the same year. After parts of the roof collapsed, killing two workmen, it was decided to pull the rest down and start again. This was achieved by two locomotives pulling on chains attached to supports resulting in 'the crashing ironwork giving out millions of sparks'. Under the two-arched new train shed, both companies retained the concept of carriage storage lines (two) between the arrival and departure lines under their 75ft wide train shed. Each company had two 640ft platforms with both arrivals flanking a central large cab road. They also had, as can be seen, their own entrances at the front of the building, two separate booking offices. By this time, the landlord had become part of the L&NWR and the 'Sheffield' had become the MS&LR. Ashton under Lyne had been ousted by places east of the Pennines on the coast. Transport was provided by 4-wheel cabs – 'Growlers'. Conveying passengers to and from the station was performed by horse drawn carriages in those days. Many drivers owned their own vehicle using two horses in rotation. It wasn't until 1896 that the Metropolitan Police introduced a driving test for horse cab-men. At the top of the road is a building that was probably the drivers' shelter; it persists throughout all of these pictures. At one time, there was a set of stairs from around the same spot, down to Store Street, which went under the approach road, almost at a right angle. Kings Cross is still advertised as a destination by the MS&LR side of the station.

1905. Although this picture was taken some forty years after the improvements, little outwardly changed during that time. The three-storey block faced a broad approach road sloping up from the street. Designed by the Manchester architects of Mills & Murgatroyd it is of the 'coarse Italianate style', however, by means of its commanding position it formed the most imposing station front in the town. It wasn't until 1877 that a town hall, denoting City status, was built. Many large stations had joint station committees to administer their business. However, as the two companies could operate their respective business separately and had little recourse to co-operate, it is not surprising that there were two station masters. On the left, towering above the street level, is the warehouse belonging to the L&NWR. Those of the GCR are behind and even more to the left. (RAS Marketing, RK Blencowe Negative Archive)

This page 1912, upper and 1937, lower. However permanent the station approach looked, internally the station wasn't. With increased business, the companies looked for room to expand. While the L&NWR had space between its departure platform and that for the branch to Altrincham (the 'MSJ' to commuters), the MS&LR was hemmed in between the L&NWR platforms and good lines to that company's Ducie Street warehouse. Ten years after the opening of the new joint station, the MS&LR used the land inside their 75ft train shed to create another platform, lettering them A, B and C which from 1882 were electrically illuminated. Platform B was the longest at 640ft, then A at 540ft with C being the shortest, just, at 530ft. The original brick offices occupied the full width of the two original train sheds: the subsequent enlargement to the L&NWR side producing the odd shaped arrangement when approaching the station. Notice that now the MS&LR has given way to the new name, Great Central Railway and that trams had arrived on the scene. The building really does dominate the view being some forty feet above London Road, on the right; little wonder the station was called, 'Top Bank' when first opened. In the last picture, reputed to be for the Coronation in 1937, the station is now part of the LNER and the LMS. Ordinary, for then, cars have come to dominate the transport scene. (Lens of Sutton Collection, BPC)

Above: **London Road interior, 1957.** After walking up the station approach, then, it is the left-hand entrance of the main building that is for MS&LR services. Either side of the gates are small huts for ticket collectors. Beyond are the buffer-stop ends of the platforms. It needs to be remembered that this side of London Road was quite a small affair, having originally only two, later expanded to three platforms, uniquely lettered, A (on the left) to C. Whereas in 1866 there were 66 arrivals and departures, this figure had swollen to 174 by the turn of the century. With the growth of services, size really did matter, and this was a contributing factor to the development of the Manchester Central Station line. A survey in 1911 showed that something less than 10 per cent of the city's daily passenger arrivals were to the GCR side of the station. (Courtesy of Manchester Libraries, Information & Archives, Manchester City Council m63050)

Opposite above: **London Road interior, 1959.** Old habits die hard. As a traveller, we have arrived into the circulating area of the joint station as if we had passed through a door on the eastern side curtain brick wall, a throwback to the entrances in the original 1840s station. Platforms are to the left and the front of the station is to the right. An official is by the cab entrance, hence the 'IN' and 'OUT' notices on the decorative columns which support the large girder, above. Like most things in the station, there were two of them. Hence to the right are the ex-L&NER refreshment rooms while on the other side of the entrance road is the ex-L&NWR establishment. Similarly, with book stalls, one had Wyman's, as seen, while our line had WH Smith, behind us. In the background is a locomotive at the end of platform 4. Although the North Staffordshire Railway ran services to London Road and they, with the MS&LR were joint owners of a line from Macclesfield, their engines only arrived here via the L&NWR line from Stockport. On the Joint line, it was the MS&LR that supplied the engines and rolling stock. (British Railways)

Platform Tickets.

A correspondent takes exception to the refusal of some of the railway companies to allow persons to accompany to the platform friends who are about to take a journey. There is something to be said for the companies, especially at this busy time of the year, when the travellers themselves sufficiently crowd the platforms, and if all were accompanied by attentive friends bidding "au revoir" the condition of things would become impossible. At the same time we think the plea that ladies and children should be permitted an escort, if only to ensure that they secure desirable company for a long journey, is one of much force. If the practice of issuing a ticket and charging a penny or twopence for the privilege of using the platform were more generally adopted, it would keep away undesirables, and would, we think, be a convenience to the public generally.—*The Globe*

Access to platforms, 1906. While we took it for granted that for the princely sum of 1d (an old penny) we as youngsters could gain access to the platforms for train-spotting, that hasn't always been the practice. (Great Central Journal, 1906)

Platform tickets, no dates. On the right is the rectangular card ticket that could be bought from the ticket office, subject to the potential questioning from the man behind the small glass opening, while on the left is the later paper version that was available from a machine on the wall. (Both BPC)

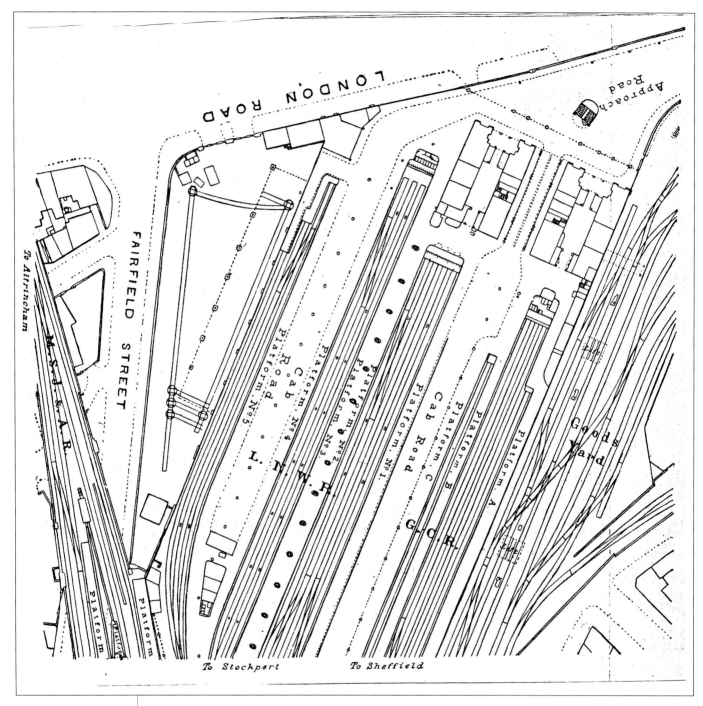

Plan, London Road, around 1900. On the right are the multiple lines that lead to both company's goods warehouses. On the GC side of the station, a two-sided line has been inserted to create platform C. Beyond the platform's ends are the two sets of office blocks with a cab road access in between them. The previous picture was taken looking through the GC booking hall and the other in the concourse looking to the left. (Railway magazine)

Roof, 1956. Above the concourse that links the office blocks with the two-train shed is a ridge and furrow glazed roof. In the background is the L&NWR extension, covering platforms 3 & 4. The details of the vents atop the train sheds show up well. (BR)

Other sides to London Road

It is easy to forget that the actual landlords of the station were the L&NWR, the 'Sheffield' were tenants, and the South Junction line was a Joint affair, to the south of the L&NWR extension.

L&NWR side of London Road

Pre-Grouping. The footplate crew pose with the train shed in the background. On either side of the approach roads to the terminus were company locomotive yards, high above Travis Street. Accessed from the joint lines, the L&NWR facilities consisted of a water tank, two stabling sidings and a turntable. 2-4-0 No 315 *Alaska* is making use of the latter. With the line to Altrincham almost exclusively operated by tank engines, this facility was particularly useful. The signals behind the engine are firstly for the joint line and the bracket post for platforms 4-7. (BPC)

Joint LNWR/GCR side of London Road. Both sets of footplate crew are intrigued by the presence of a photographer on the South Junction platform. This is a joint line running from the station throat at London Road (South Junction) to Ordsall Lane thus connecting tow points of the L&NWR empire in the city. On the right are the L&NWR platforms at London Road and just making an appearance on the extreme right is the train shed over the GC platforms. Today's H&S would have a real issue with the ladder at such an angle. The train is waiting as it has to cross over all the lines from the train sheds at the station's throat if it is to progress east. Today this manoeuvre is still a major headache for track managers.

Manoeuvres

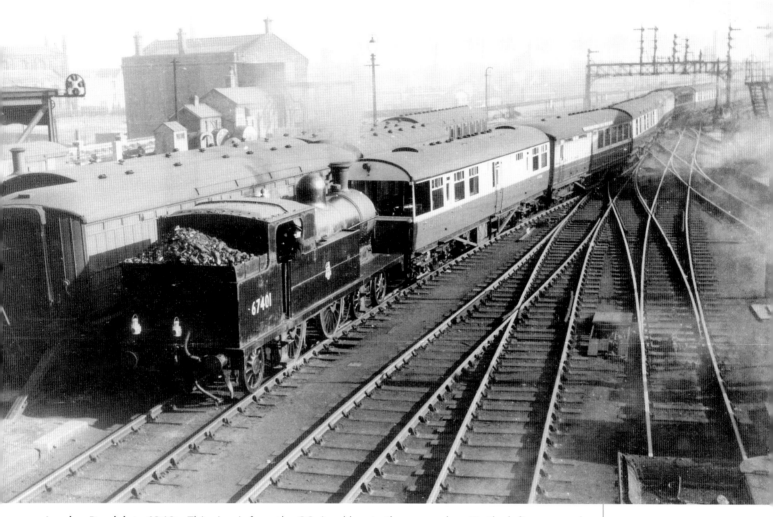

London Road, late 1940s. This view is from the GC signal box to the approaches. On the left are several general utility coaches in the two short carriage sidings, with a few sheds and brick buildings in the former GC locomotive servicing area beyond. Dragging a long train of coaches into platform A is C13 class 4-4-2T No 67401, most likely from carriage sidings at Ardwick. The engine is looking spick and span, probably fresh from a spell in Gorton works in April 1948 when it acquired the shown number. The name-boards on the roof of the coaches probably indicates its distant destinations, whether there is a train engine at the far end is impossible to determine. (E Oldham Coltas Trust)

London Road, 1940. Problems at busy termini stations revolve around lack of space and pathways for movements. Trains, having arrived, need their stock to be removed for servicing and storage, until needed. The train engine then must depart to, perform the same operations. For the L&NWR side of the station these activities happened at Longsight, a few miles south. And then for departures, the same problems, but in reverse, occur. One way of reducing engine pathways was for them to be attached, as 'passengers', to the stock they will eventually haul. The whole cavalcade, the tank engine pulling the coaches and engine, head north into a platform at London Road station. There the coaches will be detached from the tank engine and the express for passing this very spot but going the other way. The LNER adopted such practices during the war. So, an express from Marylebone has arrived into London Road. In all probability a class C tank has attached to the rear and is hauling the coaches to Ardwick for servicing with a little assistance from the train engine, A1 Pacific No 2554 *Woolwinder*. (E Oldham)

Passenger facilities at London Road

London Road, around 1890. By this time, the passenger accommodation for the 'Sheffield' company had been enlarged. This picture is of an engine, a Parker class 3, 2-4-2 No 592, at platform A with the boundary wall behind. The two men are on the inserted platform, B, which has two faces and we are on the old arrivals platform, now C. (Brian Longbone collection)

Opposite below: **MS&LR train shed, no date.** While not the best of pictures it is included as it shows the company facilities soon after the construction of their third platform in 1876. On the right is the platform for departure trains; that on the left is for arrivals. Supporting the train shed is the curtain wall, on the right, and a set of columns on the extreme left. Beyond the latter was a cab road followed by arrival and departure platforms for the landlord, the L&NWR. The sidings in between the two platforms are still inhabited by coaches. The development of the third platform coincided with the arrival of the Midland Railway. Their London trains departed from the MS&LR side of the station, going to King's Cross as St. Pancras wasn't open until the next year, making London Road very congested. Soon after, a census showed that 450 trains each day were using London Road. The limitations of the small size of their station was apparent. So much so, that they gave the MR three years notice to quit in 1875, which ultimately resulted in the development of Central station. For all the grandeur of the road approach to London Road, the MS&LR's provision was, at best, 'modest'. (BPC)

London Road, 1913. This picture was taken from the footbridge that connected the ends of all the platforms. On the right is the original train shed, now home to the GCR. On the left, is the 1866 extension, used by the L&NWR, note the iron railings separating the two. The engine is in their platform 1 and on the left, above the company livered coaches, are the double row of columns denoting the place where the further extensions would be; gaily painted they feature to this day and are seen on the rear cover. (BPC)

1026. London Road, 1923. Although this activity happens as often as trains departed, it was rarely photographed. C4 class 4-4-2 No 362 is backing down from Gorton to the front of some coaches in one of the station's platforms. This Robinson engine was built between 1903-6 and its 6ft 9in driving wheels will be put to good use at the head of a train for London. Of interest is the lettering on the tender. At the onset of the Grouping the company called itself, 'L&NER', only later to lose the '&'. A survey, in 1904, called the GCR 'one of the leading and most enterprising lines in the country'. It was famous for its handsome locomotives, clean carriages, prompt passenger trains and the extensive position of connecting services in conjunction with other companies. In addition, the provision of a buffet car at least, or a restaurant car on all daytime expresses was a clear advantage. While the landlord (L&NWR) and tenant (MS&LR) had their origins in the 1840s, well over a century later and there still existed a sense of superior and lesser being between the two sets of admin. staff who ran things from the same building in the Nationalised era. (JGD Whitaker Collection)

Opposite below: **Ex-MS&LR train shed, 1945.** Standing near the extended end of old platform C (the original MS&LR arrival platform), looking back to the city shows the end glazing the worse for 80 odd years wear and tear, not to mention two world wars. However, when first used in 1866 this must have been a magnificent spectacle, especially as it was only half the story, with a similar train shed, for the L&NWR, to the left. Still occupying the MS&LR departure line, with a train for Sheffield at least, as at opening, hauled by B7 class 4-6-0 No 5478; note the lettering on the tender. This line from platform A leads directly onto the up main line. On the extreme right are wagons occupying sidings masking the lines to both company's goods depots with the roof of the L&NWR Ducie Street warehouse above them. A short siding was built into platform C to allow a station pilot to be located between duties. Class C13 4-4-2T No 5020 gets admiring glances from young enthusiasts, or are they for the express? It is unlikely that any of the small number of schoolboys watching proceedings, strategically between the two sides of the station, had more than a pencil and a note book to record events. Behind the parachute water tank can be seen the footbridge that connected the ends of all the platforms and dates from the early 1870s. Enemy bombs in December 1940 caused major damage along the MSJ&AR and a 'nuisance' effect here, as witnessed by the missing glazing panels. (Milepost 92 ½ Railphotolibrary.com)

Leaving London Road, 1953. Mancunians were able to travel to the capital by a choice of three companies at this time. The former MR trains went from Central while the ex-L&NWR and ex-GC trains went from here. In days gone by, the GNR also ran trains to London. Fastest has always been the L&NWR as it is the shortest distance, the MR line was picturesque and allowed connections to Midlands cities as did the GC. This train, the 2.10pm for Marylebone, has LNER class V2 2-6-2 No 60831 in charge, ready to leave platform A. It is widely thought that the London Extension, with its dash & imaginative leadership, helped take the provincial MS&LR to have a renaissance as the GCR. In 1915, Robinson, the CME of the GCR first fitted his anti-collision buffers and interlocking fenders to coaches. Both were designed to minimise problems in the event of an accident. The former improved the cushion effect of buffers while the latter were intended to keep the coaches from moving laterally and to prevent telescoping in the advent of an accident. While increasing the weight of a coach by two tons, their usefulness was never tested, thankfully. (BKB Green)

Leaving London Road, 1952. Amidst the glamour of London express trains and powerful engines, it needs to be borne in mind that most of the train movements in this small terminus were of a suburban nature. Not only was there a healthy business to Hadfield and Glossop, but also along the Joint Lines to Marple, Macclesfield and Hayfield. Typical trains of their services, in early BR days, is exemplified here by C13 4-4-2T No 67417 with two coaches reversing out of the station. The engine has been altered so that the train could be driven from either end, saving time and engine movements at both ends of its journey. To perform such activities, the driver would sit in a specially adapted compartment of the rear (front) coach leaving the fireman to perform his duties on the footplate. This train has just left the platforms and is using the complex point work that joined the L&NWR tracks to the High Level goods yard and is about to pass under the magnificent signal gantry just beyond No 2 signal box (its shadow is on the right). (HF Wheeler)

Platform B, 1948. With the signal, sentry-like, guarding the right of way, B7 class 4-6-0 No 1372 (ex 5464) awaits exit from the station. Built at Vulcan Foundry in 1921 it is now based at Darnall with only six months of life left; the engine never carried a BR number. The narrow platform has side B, squashed in between the original arrival/departure platforms, by the engine: we are standing on platform C served by the line in the bottom right hand corner. The debris on the ground, left, is at the base of a parachute water tank. On the right is likely to be a lamp hut. In these days, lamps were lit by paraffin. Regularly, twice per week, the lamps were gathered from the many signals in the area. They were extinguished, the wicks cleaned, and the glass spectacle cleaned with an abrasive, pumice stone. After re-filling they were replaced, and the glass cleaned. This duty was often given to new recruits, performing between 100-120 such duties per day. One such area was from here to Ashburys East. What a wonderful job if one earned enough to have a camera! (HC Casserley)

Opposite: **Leaving London Road, early 1950s.** This picture was taken from No 2-signal box, perched above the tracks that lead to some of the L&NWR platforms, looking across to the former MS&LR side of the station. Making a spirited start from platform A is an express, probably for London, with grimy A3 Pacific 4-6-2 No 60107 *Royal Lancer* in charge. The engine has just passed a small tank engine on one of the two carriage sidings, with a similar engine on the right, on the lines that lead to the L&NWR warehouse. Above the latter is one of the wagon hoist that enabled wagons to be lowered to facilities underneath the station, at road level. (R McCarthy)

Above: **London Road station throat, 1948.** While for most railway historians the focus of the picture is one of the engines that took part in the locomotive trials at the onset of nationalisation, for us, it is the signal bridge that the train is passing under. This wonderful construction straddling the company's lines cost the landlord (the L&NWR) £228 when operational from 31 October 1909. On the right are three posts, one for each platform with the train being directed into platform 'C'. On the left are posts for up trains, goods and main line. The smaller arms and those on the shorter posts are from the carriage sidings, between platform 'A' and the L&NWR goods lines, and the carriage sidings between platforms 'A' and 'B'. (W Lees)

Opposite above: **London Road station throat, 1953.** On the left, partially hidden by a tank engine performing station pilot duties for the ex-LMS side of the station, is the controlling signal box with 62 levers, a line to a horse dock passing under it. Adjacent to it, but out of our sight, are the domed cylinders for the system as it was operated by low pressure pneumatics. The line on the left is the down main. In an attempt, from 1948, to not only have track circuits but also semaphore arms to be of the upper quadrant variety, the down posts were reduced to one, hence the gap on the gantry. These signals were replaced by a small theatre route indicator, small arms to the left-hand post and a single arm, 33ft above rail level. All these now controlled movements to the platforms, the horse dock, platform sidings and carriage sidings. The middle arm is a 'calling on' arm which was used so that an engine could access a line already occupied, for removing coaches for example. The tangle of lines immediately in front of us, leads from a shunting neck ('Middle Siding') behind us and leads to a ladder of tracks across all the running lines and onto the quadruple lines for the L&NWR goods facilities. Note the wagon hoist, complete with indicator disc, in the middle background. 'Middle siding' continues on behind us, almost up to No 1 box before merging with the up main line: the line just to our right. Veering from it, to the right, accesses the engine servicing area for the GC, almost mirroring that for the L&NWR by South Junction. The pair of lines further right are the L&NWR goods lines with the GC's pair to the right of the gantry but controlled by the solitary signal on the extreme right of the gantry. In the background is the train shed over the ex-GC platforms, dwarfed by the two company's goods provisions. (F. Shaw Collection, courtesy G. Plant)

Opposite below: **Ardwick viaduct, 1953.** There are actually two junctions at Ardwick on the viaduct south of London Road. The oldest, which we are standing on, to the right, is the 1841 main line to Sheffield, leaving the L&NWR line to Crewe, on the left. The branch, ex-L&Y 2-4-2T No 50644 is traversing with a RCTS Railtour, is the later 1848, L&Y link to their system at Miles Platting. Although not doubled until 1865, the line was advertised by the L&Y as a route for connections from Oldham, Bury and Rochdale with London bound trains at Ardwick station, the company having a platform there for this purpose. This interchange was stopped by the L&NWR from 2 December 1902, all traffic being handled at London Road instead. (N. Harrop)

Above: **Viaduct approach/exit from London Road, 1953.** With its multiple tracks high up on a viaduct, today it is hard to appreciate the fact that originally only two tracks were built, those to the west. In March 1861 the landlord (L&NWR) and tenant (MS&LR) had reached agreement concerning the widening from Ardwick Junction for the final ¾ of a mile to London Road. The MS&LR was to have exclusive use of a new pair of lines to be built to the east, giving up any normal use of the old pair that the L&NWR were to use. Crossovers enabled both companies to use each other's lines in special circumstances. Access across the L&NWR line enabled the MS&LR trains to use the South Junction Railway (they were partners in this Joint Line) was also agreed upon. Adding to the complexity is the fact that both companies had their goods warehouses to the east of London Road station. This picture shows the six running lines just before the four more branches off to serve the goods warehouses. Showing lamps to indicate a stopping train, class C14 4-4-2T No 67440 is probably heading east with a Macclesfield or Hayfield service. The MS&LR only used the two lines on the right, controlled by the four signal posts on the right. The extreme right post is for trains like ours on the up line while the fourth is for the down main line, the two in between are for the goods lines ahead. All the rest of the arms on this impressive signal bridge are for the L&NWR operations, goods lines, train station, South Junction or Mayfield's platforms. Overhead masts indicate the shape of things to come. (N. Harrop)

Opposite: **Ardwick, 1849.** Prior to the coming of the railways in 1842, a guide book for Manchester spoke of the district in glowing terms. 'Ardwick Green .... is one of the most pleasant villages in the kingdom and is universally admired for the beauty of its appearance and the neatness of its buildings.' All this was about to be shattered with the arrival of two lines across the rooftops. While the L&NWR's viaduct consists of a series of arches, just wide enough to take the pair of lines, the MS&LR approach is on an embankment with access points. Almost fifty years into the future and it would accommodate the quadrupling. Next to the station's entrance is a yard belonging to Dunkirk coal merchants; their product hasn't come far, just the few miles from their mines in the Dewsnap area. Note the milestone, 'Manchester 1 mile' to the right. (Crown Copyright: Godfrey Edition)

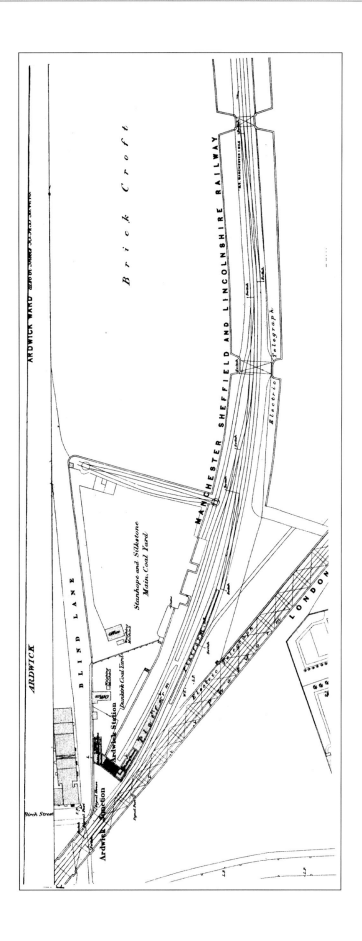

Ardwick, entrance 1963. Less than imposing is this entrance on Blind Lane. Inside was a waiting/booking hall and toilet facilities. Covered steps lead up to the platform where a footbridge, from which the next picture was taken, accesses the down platform. To illustrate the importance of freight trains, a survey taken over two days at Ardwick Junction at the start of 1857 showed that the MS&LR had more goods than passenger trains both arriving and leaving. It also showed the company provided 43 per cent of the trains with the L&Y providing a small percentage too. It wasn't until 1867 that the MR was given permission to use the MS&LR side of London Road. The ensuing competition made the landlord (L&NWR) very angry. In modern times, the station is one of the biggest success stories in the area. In the last five years its 'footfall' has doubled, beating all (bar Fairfield & New Mills Central) its neighbours. However, before the reader gets impression that vast crowds are flocking to Ardwick's platforms, it only attracted 668 passengers! Unless the nearby regeneration breathes life into the station, it must be a candidate for closure. A 20mph speed limit is imposed on trains through the station. (Courtesy of Manchester Libraries, Information & Archives, Manchester City Council m63418)

Ardwick, 1949. Arriving to connect with the L&NWR lines, about three quarters of a mile south of London Road, is a facing junction with a pair of rails heading east: these are on the viaduct in the right background. This is the L&Y's Ardwick Branch with a Board School beyond. The line to Sheffield diverges east, while the L&NWR line continues south to Longsight. The latter lines are controlled by the box to the left, Ardwick Junction, while the MS&LR lines proper have Ardwick No 1 box, just behind us, performing that task. In the very early days, there was only one down line from here into London Road. Consequently, it was the scene of bitter rivalry between the landlord (L&NWR) and tenant (MS&LR) for the right of way into the station. Until the quadrupling of the lines this competition led to much bad feeling and action/counter action between the two as can be imagined. Although the station opened in November 1842, it was re-built according to 1861 plans with platforms to be 300ft long. Passenger protection was afforded by the canopy with a waiting room at the far end. The point-work the engine is about to go over is the commencement of a pair of goods lines with access to carriage sidings, and an extensive goods yard. (J. Davenport Initial Photographics)

Ardwick, 1946. Fresh from the workshops just along the line is LNER class N4 0-6-2T No 9226. Built in 1890 as a MS&LR engine to a design of Parker it was rebuilt by Robinson with a Belpaire boiler in 1921. Due to space restrictions at Ducie Street, the company developed an extensive goods yard on bounded by the carriage sidings on the main line, the L&Y's Ardwick branch and the MR's branch that served their Ancoats goods station. Engines such as these performed shunting duties there handling coal, general goods as well as cattle. (GCRS)

Opposite above: **Ardwick, 1953.** Two men pass the time of day on the up platform as a stopping-everywhere-bar-here! train sweeps through the station. Of interest is the low height of the platform and the station's name carved into the bench. C14 class 4-4-2T No 67443 will, in a few minutes, pass where it was built, Beyer, Peacock in 1907. It differs from the often viewed C13 class in having a greater coal and water capacity. General expansion of the network led to the quadruplicating of the lines from Ardwick Junction to Priory Junction, Gorton which cost £44,000 was brought into use from 12 November 1865. This was extended forty years later, in 1905/6, to Hyde Junction. (N. Harrop)

Opposite below: **Ardwick, down platform, 1948.** The re-siting of this platform when the re-building and extension of the platforms led to it being devoid of anything other than lamps, with the name etched into the glass, and a name-board. Sparse as this appears, few, if any passengers would board trains here for the short trip to London Road and most passengers would be alighting. If passengers had to wait for a train, it would be on the up platform, hence its canopy and facilities. B1 class 4-6-0 No 61316 sets off east passed the carriage sidings; the sharpness of the curve can be gleaned by the necessity of a check rail on the down line. Above the carriages on the right are the fine lattice signals for the coalescence of the goods lines onto the main lines. Note the practise of using white discs above lamps to denote the type of train it was for signalmen. (BPC)

Above: **Ardwick sidings, 1954**. Although there were two carriage sidings outside the train shed at London Road as well as three between platforms 'A' and 'B', this was insufficient to perform the cleaning and stabling necessary for the train movements at the station. Consequently, land to the north of the main line at Ardwick was laid out for the storage and maintenance of carriages. It was here that trains were broken up and made up and then the whole train pulled into the terminus. Languishing in the sidings is clerestory carriage no E599E, a 50ft composite and luggage vehicle, built fifty years ago at Gorton. (H.C. Casserley)

Left: **Advert, 1900**. John Ashbury moved his carriage factory, founded in 1837 at Knott Mill in the centre of Manchester, to Ardwick and after the opening of the line, here in 1846. The factory, north of the line, built most of its rolling stock and coaches for the adjacent railway company before the GC opened its Dukinfield works in 1912. (Bradshaw's Railway Manual, Shareholders' Guide & Directory, 1900)

Ancoats and Ardwick branches

Neither of these branches were built by the MS&LR nor were they joint lines with other companies. However, both branches had a profound effect on the areas they ran through, the goods facilities emanating from them and the effect on services along the MS&LR, hence their inclusion. The Ancoats branch was a Midland Railway construction while the Ardwick branch was of Lancashire & Yorkshire origin. The two branches met at Midland Junction.

Ardwick Branch, 1953. We witnessed Ex-L&Y 2-4-2T No 50644 leaving Ardwick Junction a few minutes ago. Having proceeded on another viaduct it is now heading north towards another Ardwick Junction, at Miles Platting on a RCTS Railtour of Manchester district on 26 July. On the left is the MR branch from Ancoats Junction, just west of Ashburys station. This picture was taken a short time before the 'knitting' went up; it only extended for a short distance north of here. (C.H.A. Townley)

Ardwick branch, 1951. If some readers are having a sense of, 'I've seen this engine before,' then they may well be correct; it latterly resided at the Keighley & Worth Valley Railway. Andrew Barkley built 0-4-0ST No 4 *R. Walker* is pictured at Bradford Road gas works, just north of the crossing the Manchester & Ashton under Lyne canal accessed from the east of the branch. Prior to the colliery being rail connected, most of its output had been consumed locally by households, small businesses with some being loaded onto barges on the adjacent canal. Work started in 1944 to increase production and a tunnel was built so that a conveyer belt could be used to supply a near-by power station at Stuart Street. Not surprisingly, subsidence in such a built-up area caused the pit to close, despite there being substantial coal reserves. (Alex Appleton)

Ardwick branch, 1953. The Manchester & District Railtour on 7 July has not long left London Road station and has arrived on L&Y metals via Ardwick and Midland Junctions. It is signalled, from Philips Park box, to pass onto the L&Y's Ashton branch to continue its tour. The gas-holders belong to Bradford Road works. Some of the coal for the works had not travelled far as south of the works was the Beswick branch with connections to Bradford colliery. The branch was a convenient route for excursions to Belle Vue from Bradford and other L&Y towns, as well as cross city freight trips e.g. to Ordsall Lane. (C.H.A. Townley)

ASHBURYS. GCR.

Ashburys station, around 1910. East of Ardwick and the line climbs at 1 in 173 for the next two miles as far as Gorton. About a mile from Ardwick and as the line crosses Pottery Lane, a small station was opened in July 1855. The suffix 'for Openshaw' appeared in the November edition of Bradshaw only to change to 'for Belle Vue' in the August of the next year. The name comes from a nearby wagon builder who paid £175 for the station's erection, initially, only the Stalybridge branch trains stopping there. Quite when the apostrophe disappeared is unknown. Looking back towards Manchester shows the main station buildings on the side for London Road: the photographer is stood just across the bridge over Pottery Lane. Posing on the down platform are some of the station staff and of interest is the milk churn in the pre-refrigeration days. Being one of the stations close to the pleasure gardens at Belle Vue, the name-boards told strangers they were there. At the end of the up platform was this magnificent signal gantry. The three left hand posts are for the down fast line, on the left. The other two posts are for the down slow line which is behind us, to the right. At the end of the station were two junctions at Ashburys West: to Ardwick sidings and to Ancoats goods depot as well as to the L&Y branch. (Lens of Sutton)

Ashburys station, 1939. Standing on the platform for a trip to Manchester shows an equally magnificent signal gantry at the eastern end of the station. The down platform, accessed by a subway, was Spartan to say the least! Notice the practise of writing the name of the station into the glass on the lamps. On the right, oddly, the ladies waiting room was separate from the main building which had the gents. lavatory at this end. The backdrop is made up of a familiar east Manchester skyline; factories and smoke from chimneys. To the left are the up/down slow lines and ahead are routes controlled by East Junction box, vaguely visible under the station's awning. As indicated by the up-bracket signal, for the fast lines, the main route is straight on towards Gorton with the minor route being south towards Belle Vue along the Joint Line. For trains on the slow line the options were straight ahead or accessing the reception lines and Ashbury's sidings. (Stations UK)

Ashburys sidings. On the north side of the line were extensive sidings where goods trains were tripped to other places in the region. March 1960. Soon to be replaced by the ubiquitous 08 diesel shunter is locally based (Gorton, 9G) J11 class 0-6-0 No 64363. These Robinson Great Central class J11 engines had been doing their vital, but humble work since introduction in 1901. (A Swain)

April 1951. Looking across the bridge over Pottery Lane shows Gorton based N5 class 0-6-2T No 69260 shunting on the goods lines. Above the engine is a set of signals operated by the signalman in Ashburys East Junction box via levers 27 (bottom) to 29-which always seems to be 'off' in all illustrations it appears in. (H.C. Casserley)

Junctions east of Ashburys

Ashburys East Junction, 1953. Just getting into its stride is V2 Class 2-6-2 No 60890. Its train, a respectable eight coaches, is the 2.10pm to Marylebone, wouldn't be able to compete with the much shorter timings on the MR and even shorter times on L&NWR trains, but did allow connections to Sheffield and the East Midlands. The train is passing over the junction with the MR/MS&LR Joint Line controlled by the 32-lever box visible above the third coach. (B.K.B. Green)

Below: **Priory Junction, 1952.** Around seven hundred yards to the east and this 64-lever signal box, on the left, controlled the main access to massive railway infra-structure complex at Gorton. Its levers also looked after a crossover between the fast and slow lines. Making such a manoeuvre is B1 class 4-6-0 No 61157 as it takes the 10.25am to London Marylebone on 17 August. The wonderful lattice signal gantry informs trains on the down slow about their intended route: the two arms on the right for the reception lines of Ashbury's sidings. In the background is the coaling tower of the engine shed here. (B.K.B. Green)

Gorton

All accounts of the line, under whichever management, would be incomplete without doing justice to this district of Manchester, even though the works were actually situated in the adjacent settlement of Openshaw! However, an account of the line must have perspective. So, while a whole book could be, and probably has been, written about the area, its people and its engines, we will have to make do with a fleeting glimpse. Having roots in Meadow Street, Ancoats, I wish there was room for more. So important to the country's war efforts was this area that the German air force produced maps, translated into German, indicating targets for bombing.

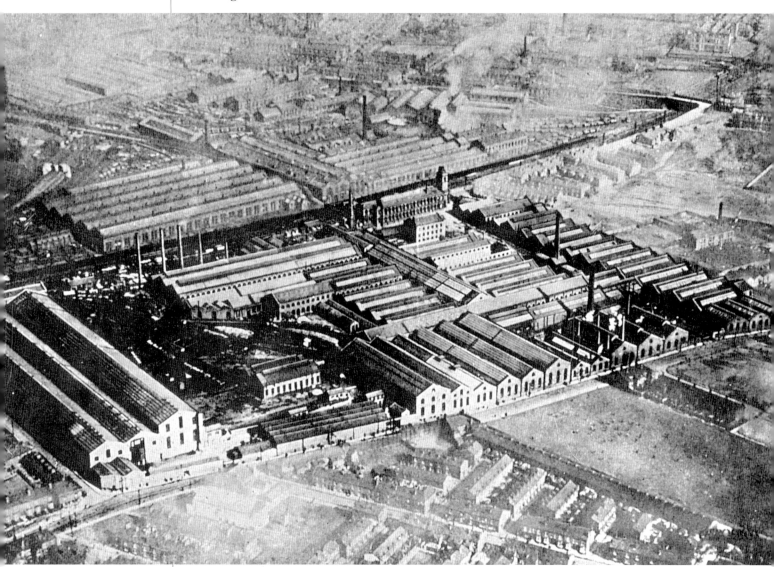

Beyer, Peacock & Co. Ltd. (Aerial view) While most readers will be familiar with the MS&LR's establishment on the up side of the main line, few will have any idea that literally, across the line, was the locomotive works of Beyer, Peacock, dating from 1854. Almost fifty years later in 1902, now as part of the Workshop of the World, it employed 2,000 men and covered 22 acres. (Joe Lloyd Collection)

Beyer, Peacock products. Richard Peacock and Charles Beyer set up this factory making engines for British railways. About ⅔ of their output was for export, the most famous being the Beyer-Garrett style which were used successfully in many countries such as Argentina, Australia and South Africa. This example was for Tanganyika Railways. (Joe Lloyd Collection)

Beyer, Peacock product, 1925. Under construction is the unique engine No 2395, ironically, destined for the LNER. The front engine is well advanced and the rear unit is awaiting, amongst other things, the tender. (W Potter Collection, Kidderminster Railway Museum)

Gorton works

No mention of Gorton would be complete without a reference to the locomotive works there. The main line was sandwiched between heavy engineering works. To the south was Beyer, Peacock whilst on the opposite side of the line was with Armstrong Whitworth and the MS&LR works. Having its origins around 1848, the latter were expanded and incorporated an engine shed, employing some 6,222 workers in 1902. After the Grouping, the LNER decided to concentrate locomotive construction at other centres like Darlington and Doncaster leaving Gorton to specialise on repair work. British Rail gave the contract for the construction of its 57 EM1 electric engines to Gorton from 1950 and a few years later for the EM2 class to be built there too. With the BR works closing in 1962 and those of Beyer, Peacock four years later the loss of so many jobs had a devastating effect on the area.

Erecting shop, 1938. The mechanism for repairing, and building locomotives was rather simple, in theory! Several tank engines are in different states of repair, 5168 is on the left. An engine was craned into a vacant place in the shop, placed on jacks and stripped of all its parts. Hopefully, these were all carefully numbered! Any defective parts were replaced, others repaired and cleaned. Finally, just like a new engine, all the pieces were put back together again – with none over! (BPC)

Before, 1948. Standing in lines with parts cannibalised for scrap or for re-use on other engines, new or repair, are a series of engines. B9 4-6-0 No 1471 is nearest. Forty-two years ago and its parts were probably in this form, ready to be melted down in the establishment south of the main lines. Note the pile of chairs in between the rows, probably ready for recycling. (H.C. Casserley)

After, 1925. Fresh from construction is Robinson designed 4-6-2T No 5045. While the LNER policy was to paint all tank engines black, there were exceptions. The livery would be green with red (or orange) lining. Intended for fast suburban stopping passenger trains e.g. on the Marylebone to Aylesbury services, they were often used here, locally, on Macclesfield trains. A feature of the last two batches of 10 + 13 engines were the side windowed cabs. Note the screen over the 4tons bunker. On the extreme left is part of the colloidal fuelling plant referred to in a London Road picture. (BPC)

Making the works work

While there is no shortage of illustrations of stripped down engines, there are few that show the daily routine jobs.

***Above*: Crane, no date.** To assist in the removal of parts of engines most railway companies altered a small tank (1903) to provide that extra bit of muscle. Being of short wheel base, there would be few places they couldn't reach, doubly so with the crane in the coal bunker. No 889 is a modified 0-6-0ST with the addition of a trailing axle due to the extra weight (4tons). Note the bell by the cab to warn workers of their presence. Just after the end of the Great War 'Little Dick' was converted back to its original format. (BPC)

***Opposite above*: Moving the goods, 1948.** Here, LNER 0-6-0ST No 8065 is pushing a wagon with, '*Shunt Wagon Gorton*,' on the side. On it would be parts form another engine on its way to another part of the works. In the background is a selection of small carts and trolleys used for moving small articles. (H.C. Casserley)

***Opposite below*: Gorton Loco. Yard signal box, 1949.** On the right is one of the abutments for the bridge over Bessemer Street. Heading off to the left is the exit line from Ashburys sidings, beyond, and the up slow line, behind us. Backing towards the massive shed is LNER J11 0-6-0 No 4346; the space in-front of the railwayman is where the old coaling stage was. Controlling movements around this potentially dangerous crossing is this 1928 replacement for an earlier, 1906, signal box with 41 levers. The 'Lighthouse' became redundant from 1934 when a replacement coaling shed was opened which reduced tremendously the amount of movement in the yard. It became a store and a base for the Senior Running Foremen. They directed the Passed Cleaners to deputise as firemen to cover sickness or special workings. (Millbrook House Ltd.)

Gorton shed, pre-1897. The site for the MS&LR's engine shed, in Openshaw, two miles from London Road was determined by being beyond the taxation reach of Manchester, level land, canals to bring raw materials and a nearby supply of labour. The establishment of many staff houses and a reservoir, capable of holding a month's supply of water, is probably the origin of the nickname Gorton earned – 'The Tank'. In the early 1850s, a circular shed, capable of holding seventeen tender engines around a forty-foot turntable was built. Illustrating the growth of the 'villages' in the area are the population figures for Gorton. Every decade from 1851-1871, the population more than doubled, and by the latter date, Openshaw had merged with Manchester. Expansion of the company resulted in a new shed being built to the east of Bessemer Street in 1877. This was a straight shed capable of holding ninety locomotives and cost a staggering £36,000. A wide variety of engines are in view. These range from 4-4-0 express engines, 0-6-0 tender engines and suburban passenger 2-4-2T engines, all with MS&LR logo. Note the breakdown train ready and waiting. (BPC)

On Turntable, 1949. Having not long received its BR number is Thompson re-build O1 class 2-8-0 No 63590 being turned. Starting off with one, beyond the original coaling stage, this was 60ft. A petrol driven one of 64ft 10in was added in 1905, to the east of the running shed. After being constructed by the North British Loc. Co. in 1912, it was assigned the number 1243 by the GCR. Re-numbering by the LNER saw the number 6243 and in 1944 it was re-built, (different boiler, higher pressure, Walschaerts valve gear and new cylinders) and two years later carried No 3590. (BPC)

Coaling stage, around 1920s. In 1927 there were about 200 engines allocated here and so the job of coaling all these must have been a logistical nightmare, eventhough there was this double-sided coaling facility. Loaded coal wagons were pushed up two lines in the centre and their contents man-handled into engines' coal space via steel tubs. To the side of the building was a 60ft turntable where the engines progressed. After turning, as witnessed by the engine on the left, they then used a different track to pass to behind us and then went forward into the shed area. In-front of each shed road was a pit into which ash was disposed of: around 250 tons of this had to be removed every week. (John Ryan Collection)

Gorton shed, 1938. Construction of new workshops and carriage sheds took place in the 1890s and, like the MR in Derby, the GNR in Doncaster and the GWR in Swindon, the company developed facilities for employees, here a school. Continual growth of business resulted in the carriage and wagon side heading east to Dukinfield: there had been a wagon repair shop there at Dog Lane some fifty years ago. The space vacated at Openshaw became a vast erecting shed while the running shed now with twenty roads, was capable of accommodating 120 engines by 1910, having two turntables. In view is 4-6-0 No 6326, 0-6-2T no 5543 and 2-4-2T Nos 5776 and 5594. Note power cables across the roof. (W. Potter)

Gorton, 1948. At its peak, around 1,000 men worked here, most (about 700) as drivers and firemen, approx. 250 repair and shed staff, 30 or so in the offices and 30 to 40 cleaners. Cleaning O4 class 2-8-0 No E3611 is such a team. One of the cleaners' key tasks was to ensure that the engines for their crack London trains, especially the 3.50pm, was immaculate. Their working week would be 48 hours, 8 until 4.30pm during the week and for five hours, starting at 6am., on Saturday. As with drivers, there was a pecking order amongst cleaners. The youngest lads collected materials from the stores and worked as directed, the junior workers worked on the wheels, motion and boiler while the senior cleaner applied himself to the footplate. The liquid used was of unknown composition, probably mostly paraffin, and the used cloths were collected and squeezed. The cloths were re-used and the resultant liquid put into barrels which was used by the Permanent Way staff for oiling points. Cleaners, upon examination, could become 'Passed Cleaners' and so could work on the footplate. (H.C. Casserley)

View from coaling tower, no date. In 1932, the manual coaling stage was demolished and a mechanical concrete coaling tower, closer to the main line, built. We are looking east from the top of this structure. On the right are the quadruple main lines with Priory Junction signal box next to the chimney. On the left is Openshaw goods shed. The engine appears to be drawing out from underneath us, empty coal wagons while there are three sidings of full replacements, ready to be fed into our structure. Directly beneath us are the wet ash disposal lines with wagons, on the right, with the product. The pits were emptied by a grab crane into wagons in an adjacent siding, usually on a weekend morning. This effectively stopped the smooth running of the shed and if any problem occurred, could cause congestion. When full, the rake of 24 wagons, were sent to Ashburys Bottom End, waiting to be taken to Dinting Tip for emptying. (John Ryan Collection)

Inset: Ash pit duty. Prior to the installation of mechanical facilities here, and as at many sheds, the fire was dropped into a pit. When it was safe, men simply stood in the pit and shovelled the ash out and another team moved it into wagons for disposal. Getting staff was a real problem for BR in the 1950s and with 'cleaner' production jobs at local factories, one can see why. (BPC)

Gorton, around 1900. A down train is passing through the station with its low platforms, a legacy from its beginnings on 23 May 1842, a mile east of Ashburys station. At the opening of the line the previous year, there was simply a single line but this restriction on operations meant that the doubling of the line and the opening of the station probably happened around the same time; doubtless small wooden buildings sufficed. Three years later, in anticipation of the completion of the line between Manchester and Sheffield, permanent buildings were authorised (with the same contractor doing likewise at Mottram and Newton, all for £1,600). It was sandwiched between over-bridges carrying Cornwall Street (to the west) and the Stockport branch of the Manchester & Ashton-under-Lyne canal. Passenger access was down a ramp from the booking office which was on Chapman Street (the continuation of Cornwall Street south of the line), next to the Station Hotel. Note the up signal on the 'wrong' side of the line with the background painted white to aid sighting on the bricks of the bridge. The engine is GCR 4-4-0 No 707. In 2012, we are back to this situation, two lines, again. (R.K. Blencowe Collection)

Gorton & Openshaw, 1948. As part of the desire to increase capacity along the line here, the tracks were quadrupled in 1905/6 from Ardwick Junction to Priory Junction, west of Gorton station which cost £44,000. This was extended in 1905/6 to Hyde Junction. This is the finished article, opening on 25 August 1906, looking west towards the canal bridge, with its new name. There are now four lines and platform faces; we are standing on the down main, the lines paired by speed. Passenger access to the station was down two long ramps, one either side of the tracks, connected by the fine metal footbridge, complete with ornate lamp. At the end of this platform and the signal box is visible on the original. The measure of passenger protection for a small urban station may seem excessive, however, services were in direct competition with trams by this time. I wonder how many pupils in the Bingley Street Board school, up on the right, had been told of for watching movements down in the station? They could have looked out of the windows to the north to look at the goings on in the Atora suet works! (H.C. Casserley)

Gorton & Openshaw, exterior, front and rear, 1962. Lees Street was widened north of its crossing of the line to produce a waiting place for vehicles. This uninviting and uninspiring collection of huts contained the station's facilities. They were of wooden construction, with a corrugated iron skin. Looking up from the platforms shows the rear of the street entrance, rather Tardis like – its front belies its actual size. Sturdy brick piers support them all. After purchasing a ticket, passengers walked down either of the two ramps which flanked the lines to platform 1 & 4. A set of steps led down from the footbridge that connected the two ramps with the island platforms, 2 & 3. (Both G. Whitehead)

Gorton & Openshaw, down shelter, 1962. This rather fine waiting room with large canopy was on platform 4. Note the provision for bikes, on the left and the buckets in case of fire. On the right is the ramped exit at which a ticket collector would appear when a train from Manchester arrived. There was a more extensive shelter on this platform, on the right in the previous panorama. The company reasoned that passengers using the station would be travelling towards in equal numbers in both directions, hence the platform provision was similar. (G. Whitehead)

Fairfield, 1950. Opening with the section of the line to Godley, was, at that time, the first station out of Manchester, the delightfully, and appropriately, named, 'Fairfield'. It was just over ¾ of a mile east of Gorton, when it was built, with gradient stiffening, now up at 1 in 100. The two-platform affair, complete with station master's house, after the original single line was doubled, was at the southern end of Station Road, itself a branch of Ashton Old Road. Five years later, in 1846, for the modest sum of £94, Henry Worth of Sheffield constructed station buildings there, lasting for over fifty years in this state. With the original station site having been passed almost three hundred yards and half a minute ago, the train is now passing through the district's second station, with street access from buildings on Booth Street, above the rear of the train. The station's name boards proclaim, 'Fairfield for Droylsden', the latter being a little to the north. Working hard up the gradient is B1 class 4-6-0 B1 No 61156, passing along the original up main line, now the up fast line, as in 1905/6 the company widened the lines by the addition of a pair of slow lines to the north, on the right. This excursion would be full of excited race-goers on their way to Doncaster for the St. Leger race meeting. See map on page 193 also. (N Field/MLS)

Fairfield, exterior, 1962. When the MS&LR wanted to connect two parts of its operations at Manchester's London Road and Central, and so Liverpool, stations, it built a line through the southern suburbs of the city. Opening at the start on 1 October 1891 to Fallowfield and on 2 May the following year, the line arrived at Gorton and at Fairfield. However, to achieve the fast running of its express trains along the line, the company built the junction with the main line, and a new station, where Booth Road crossed the line, some three hundred yards east nearer Guide Bridge. The original Station Road was re-named Manshaw Road (as it was on the boundary between Manchester and Audenshaw). The station booking office was built above the island platform so created with covered ways leading to equally protected steps to the platforms where adequate canopies with small waiting shelters were provided. Notice the fancy brickwork. Inscribed in the three gables are the name, its function and the date, in the middle one, 1892. (G. Whitehead)

Fairfield, 1962

Thank goodness that Graham Whitehead had the foresight to capture this station for posterity. In 1903, a contract was let to quadruple the lines from Gorton to Guide Bridge. This involved laying two lines north of the existing main lines. Now with six platforms, the station here was the second biggest on the GC system north of Nottingham! One possible reason was, according to Speake & Witting in their History of Droylsden, 'designed to accommodate the large number of passengers who were expected for a proposed Manchester race track and football ground'. They were built elsewhere.

Platform 1

Stairs. Leaving the booking hall passengers would pass along the covered footbridge and descend these steps to arrive at the up slow platform. Interesting details are the supporting legs, the canopy over the entrance to the stairs and the lamp above it.

Shelter. This was for stopping trains to the east, such as Glossop. The '3' refers to the place where a three car, the standard length of an EMU, should stop. This would be calculated from the rear of the train next to the steps to the footbridge thereby minimising the distance passengers had to walk, very important in Manchester weather! If passengers had to wait for a train, there was this small brick shelter. There are stone lines above and below the windows. There are four pieces of ironwork to help support the canopy.

Platforms 2/3

Platform 4

Shelter. This island platform had faces to the down slow, No 2, on the far side, and the up fast No 3, this side. This is a slightly stretched and double-sided version of the shelter behind it. There were two waiting rooms, one exclusively for women. Note the gas lights. Underneath the two holiday, by rail of course, adverts are buckets to be used in-case of fire.

Buildings. The line in-front of this platform is the up fast line. The substantial building has cutely curved windows and two substantial waiting rooms, the left hand one for ladies. The BR signs say 'Fairfield for Droylsden' with the platform seats simply having the first place carved into their backrest. This is one side of another island platform. To the rear is the up Central station Loop platform. The two white stripes may well be hangovers from the blackout days in the Second World War, when such devices were used to aid sighting. An iron girder runs along the edge of the extensive saw-toothed canopy.

Audenshaw, 1925. Earlier, we saw this engine being constructed. This is the first trip that the Garrett made outside the works, 21 June, on its way to Woodhead. It is passing along the main line east of Fairfield; note the two pairs of tracks separating to accommodate a bridge's pier. Being a Sunday, not many people knew about this test trip, however, they may have thought it was just another grey engine, fresh from the works. The two coaches presumably contain various officials; the results of this test are unknown. On its return to Beyer, Peacock, the round buffers were replaced by LNER oval ones, the letters *'LNER'* were repositioned from the front tank and the rear bunker to the central frame beneath the boiler. At the end of that week it went to Doncaster, undergoing more trials. An article accompanying a picture in the *Daily Dispatch* sensationalised these events calling it, 'a giant engine burning 2 ½ tons of coal an hour'. Little did they know that this seemingly harmless piece of journalistic licence had hit the nail on the head when it came to its later life. Quite why there is a person on the front is a mystery; if he did spot anything untoward, how would he convey this to the driver? Note the down signal, above the coach, with a lower backboard to aid sighting. The Locomotive Committee of the LNER was referring to there being two Garrett engines in October 1923, in the end the company bought just this one for a lower price. (HC Casserley)

Audenshaw Junction, circa 1920. As with many towns, sighting of signals was a problem caused by over bridges, the quarter of a mile west of Guide Bridge was no exception with the line passing under a series of bridges in rapid succession. Looking towards the station shows the two arches of Audenshaw Road in the distance with two L&NWR railway bridges in-front, both carrying lines that avoided Guide Bridge station. To enable train crew to see the signals, the GCR built massive signal gantries, or signal bridges, the top arms are 55 feet above rail level. This height must have been a nightmare for the person replacing the oil in the lamps. There were lower repeater arms so that the message from the signals could be read at engine level, all operated by a small (24 levers) Audenshaw Junction signal box on the down side. The branch to the left (north) from between the second and third bridges, went to meet a line from Guide Bridge station through Ashton-under-Lyne to Oldham (the OA&GB) at Canal Junction. In the latter part of the last century the curve featured heavily in the L&Y/OA&GB competition for the Manchester-Oldham traffic. The signals were in two groups; for the slow line on the left and for the fast line on the right. In each group, the main route's post is slightly higher than the others to make it stand out better. The signals were, from left to right, up slow to branch, up slow through, up fast to branch, up fast to up slow and up fast through. The curve, and box, closed in 1938 and were removed in the war. Readers can see the frame from the signal box at the NRM at York. (John Ryan Collection)

Audenshaw Junction, 1952. With sighting problems about to be manifest from the OHW about to be erected along the line, let alone those caused by the previous signalling arrangements and over-bridges, it was decided to remove the gantry and replace the arms by ordinary colour lights on posts. (Courtesy F. Shaw, T. Moseley Collection)

Stockport Junction, early 1950s. Passing on the up fast line is an express train, hauled by an unidentified B1 class engine. There are two important lines meeting the main line west of Guide Bridge station. From the north is the line from Oldham and Ashton (lines under the rear coaches) while the branch from Stockport arrives from the south (lines under the first coach). The L&NWR's Cock Lane goods yard seems to be doing a brisk trade in timber as well as having numerous petrol tank wagons parked in it. (R. McCarthy)

Above: **Stockport Junction, 1945.** The driver is keeping a careful lookout for the signal between the platforms in the station ahead as he threads his train across both junctions. Passing on the up slow line is a van train while B7 class 4-6-0 No 5038 occupies the up fast line. Sheffield, its home shed was Darnell, may be its destination. Off to the left, subject to a strict 15mph speed limit, is the branch to Stockport, accessible from all four running lines. Equally, a hint is discernible under the first vehicle, is the branch to Oldham, also speed limit protected and reachable from all four running lines. Such a complex is under the control of the forty levers in the signal box. (H.C. Casserley)

Below: **Express services: down, 1945.** Showing the lack of maintenance during the war years by lots of steam coming from odd places, V2 class 2-6-2 No 4887 prepares to depart with the 09.56 Sheffield to Manchester three months after the war ended. This was the service from Leicester with an arrival time in London Road of 11.20am, a journey time of 84 minutes from Sheffield. The engine would become No 916 only to be renumbered 60916 in 1949. It carried this number until 1964 when it was withdrawn (June, scrapped in August). Note the massive, typical L&NWR, stop blocks in the adjacent coal sidings, the corrugated shed bearing the owner's name proudly. (H.C. Casserley)

Guide Bridge

Where the Ashton to Hooley Hill lane bridged the canal between Manchester and Ashton under Lyne, a post was erected to indicate directions hence the term 'Guide bridge'.

Guide Bridge station

It was only natural when the single line railway opened in 1841 that a station close to this crossing point of the canal be called 'Ashton & Hooley Hill'. A passing loop added soon after opening and when the branch from here to Stalybridge branch opened in 1845, the name was altered to just 'Ashton' and then changed completely to 'Guide Bridge'. The attempt by the promoters that the line really did pass through Ashton-under-Lyne was then abandoned. Although almost forgotten now, Guide Bridge was a famous and important rail cross-roads in steam days. The main line passenger station was sandwiched between junctions, in the west to Oldham (north) and Stockport (south) and in the east, to Stalybridge, extensive sidings and a short distance further along the line, to Marple.

Guide Bridge, exterior, 1906. A rare glimpse into the pre-1906 alterations. The slope serving the down side of the station is from Guide Lane, behind us. Just appearing in between, the buildings is the goods shed, across the running lines with an impressive signal gantry controlling up and down movements. Almost off the picture on the right-hand side is a small part of the footbridge that appears on so many other pictures. It carried a footpath from Hooley Hill to the towpath of the canal, right across all the railway lines. The stone buildings are soon to make way for a curve of brick structures that reflect the use of the station better. (BPC)

Guide Bridge, interior, 1906. This rather poor, but of historical interest, view is towards Manchester with Guide Lane crossing the lines. The assembled station staff are on the down platform line. Following alterations in the 1870s and later, the station had four tracks, but still only two platform faces. The 1906 plan was to increase the number of platforms by building an island platform between the pair of fast and slow lines. To achieve this, the station entrance and associated offices, on the left, had to be knocked down and new ones built some 10-15yd to the left. The pair of fast lines were then slewed to the left leaving sufficient space for an island platform to be built, approx. where the men are standing on the track. A footbridge and well as a subway connecting all platforms. Buildings on the new platform were wooden and consisted of facilities for men and women, general waiting room was constructed at the bottom of the stairs and a refreshment room. The station also boasted a news-stand. (Not on island platform though, on 1 or 4) All are men, ranging from young lads, probably about twelve, with the odd older person. The man in the bowler hat is probably the station master. The Great War in ten years' time would puncture this androgynous establishment, a little as would the next war, leading to greater equality and employment opportunities for women. A subway connected the platforms, its supports can be seen in the middle pair of lines. With so many services as well as the exchanges between trains, these two platforms probably couldn't cope. (Paul White)

Guide Bridge Station exterior, 1968. As well as new buildings at platform level, the GC re-built the Guide Lane booking office in its present form: note the attempt to have fancy brickwork. While originally it had a glass canopy over the doorway, the whole unpretentious air of the buildings was in total contrast to its grand design at other stations, given that all the main express trains stopped here and there were refreshment rooms too. The booking office led to a double footbridge, just visible on the right, which gave access to all platforms, both for passengers and for luggage, the square building houses one of the three luggage hoists. (J.P. Alsop)

Local train, 1920s. Until they were eclipsed, F class 2-4-2T engines were the mainstay of suburban services. Here, on the up main line is a train of six-wheel coaches with F1 No 5596 at the head. With its tender piled high with coal it is likely that it hasn't long been on duty from Gorton shed. Therefore, it is interesting to see that its water tanks are receiving attention. Mostly hidden by the engine is a water column. The leather, flexible hose has been put into the tank on the far side and the water wheel turned on. Now, after refilling and turning the supply off, the fireman is pulling the rope attached to the end of the metal pipe to swing the hose around to a collecting duct, on the extreme left. Fascinating to watch as this was as a schoolboy, one had to be alert to the prospect of the swinging hose spraying too inquisitive lads with water! (BPC)

Local train, 1948. More powerful engines such as this C13 class 4-4-2T superseded the 2-4-2T locomotives. Setting off from platform 3, probably for Macclesfield or Hayfield, is No 7402 with train that includes 3rd class non-corridor clerestory coaches. To assist staff when walking between the platforms is the crossing in the foreground made of old wooden sleepers, cut to fit the spaces. The goods shed is behind the train. (H.C. Casserley)

Ashton Junction, 1945. This is the 9.30am Liverpool-Hull on 15 September with LNER class B17 4-6-0 No 2872 in charge. Having backed onto the coaches in Manchester's Central station, the train will have come along the Fairfield loop to join the ex-GC main line to Sheffield. It carried this number from its building by Robert Stevenson in 1937 until 1946. Then via No 1672 it carried No 61672 until its withdrawal in 1960. The station had unique signalling at this eastern end too. Controlling the up fast line that the train is on is a four-posted lattice bracket signal with characteristic finials. The tallest post is for the most used route: up main line while the other route would be onto the up slow, up branch and finally, into the up loop. On the right are the signals controlling the up slow line, with three underslung arms to maximise sighting for train drivers. I wonder if there was ever an accident under these signals with a tall passenger? There is a signal between the up/down fast lines as a guide to the signals in-front made necessary by the curving nature of the platform-this was later replaced by a banner repeater signal just east of Guide Lane bridge. (H.C. Casserley)

Ashton Junction, 1971. Although there are OHW to clutter up the view, the signal box is essentially as built in 1906, containing 48 levers. It is at the London end of the down fast platform, to the right. On the left are a series of ten blind end storage lines: Liverpool sidings. Trying to hide underneath the steps is a vacuum cylinder necessary for the electro-pneumatic point motors. As well as overseeing the up ends of the station this box controlled the line to Stalybridge, the Liverpool sidings and two down goods lines. (M.A. King)

Signalman, early 1950s. Leaning out of the window is signalman Alec Braden. Note his attire: shirt, sleeves rolled up, tie, knitted (in cable stitch) tank top, all typical of a generation who had worked on the railway for much of their lives, with pride. (Ray McCarthy)

Goods at Guide Bridge

Cattle train, no date. Heading east along the up fast line is this short train with a GC brake van at the rear. It has just passed under a signal slung between the two platforms to give drivers advance notice of the state of the signals on the fine bracket post at this end of the station, made necessary due to the curve in the layout. The white along the bottom of the wagons is probably the extent of the lime washing they have received in an attempt to sterilise the wagons and so reduce the spread of infection. The 1933 working timetable shows a Tuesdays only train for cattle from Guide Bridge to Trafford Park Sidings at 4.45am. The engine then returns along the Central station line light, to Gorton shed, arriving at 6.35am. At 2pm an engine makes the return trip to take the 3.15pm on its way to Sheffield, which may be the train seen here. (GCRS No E66)

Foreign train, 1945. Congestion in Guide Bridge station meant that the L&NWR built avoiding lines to the west, for Oldham, and the east, for Stalybridge in the 1890s. The latter linked up two parts of its empire, at Stockport with that at Yorkshire. Liverpool trains could pass along their own lines and not be subject to the delays and payments necessary when passing over another company's lines. However, repairs to that line and eventual closure forced trains back to their original route. Here a train, about to pass under bridge No 23 – Guide Lane – heads along the up slow and platform 1. In all probability, dirty ex-L&NWR G2a class 0-8-0 No 9225 hauls yet another unfitted freight from Stockport to Stalybridge. Nationalisation has still to be discussed by politicians as the station's name proclaims its owners; history repeating itself now with Train Operating Companies being responsible for some stations. (H.C. Casserley)

Station name-board, 1950s. This was at the eastern end of the down main platform, mostly for the benefit of local traffic. There is no mention of Stockport. Ashton could be reached by trains departing from either end of the station passing to Oldham Road station or Park Parade station en route to Oldham or Stalybridge, respectively. (D Lawrence)

Views from the footbridge

West, 1951. Looking towards the station with part of Ashton Junction signal box on the left. Next to it is a dock with livestock pens. The four platform faces are clear with the curving fast ones to the left. A stopping passenger train occupies the up main line, giving off plenty of smoke. The goods lines serve the platforms on the right. The wagons on the right are in Guide Bridge goods yard with its shed just visible on the extreme right. Soon, this view will be impossible. Footbridge, No 25 will have its sides covered in to protect walkers from the possibility of reaching to touch the OHW that are imminent, hence the gantry over all the lines. (R. McCarthy)

West, late 1940s. Heading east along the up slow line is a fitted freight, destined for Dog Lane sidings or Dunford Bridge sidings. Built by the North British Loco. Co. for the Ministry of Munitions in 1918, taken into LNER traffic ten years later as No 6590 and classified as O4 class. In 1946, it was re-numbered 3785 only for BR to put a '6' at the front in 1949. On the right are the goods facilities at Guide Bridge. (J Davenport)

East, 1939. About to enter the station on the down fast line is an express with B1 Class 4-6-0 No 61182 in charge. On the right are two down slow lines with access to the adjacent Liverpool sidings just getting into the bottom right. In between these lines is a water column, indicating that trains waiting for a pathway through the station could replenish their supplies. The tall lattice post, made necessary due to the footbridge we are standing on, in the middle of the picture is for the down main line, its neighbour to the left is the up fast line. Further to the left are the pair of slow lines with the crossovers between these two pairs of lines at the edge of the picture. Facing us is a bracket signal; this is for the up slow line, the post with two arms is for the Stalybridge line. Down trains from the branch would obey the signals on the bracket above the rear coaches. In the distance are tantalising glimpses of the wonderful signals at Guide Bridge North Junction; a partially obscured signal bridge for up trains and a five-post bracket for down trains. Either side of the branch are loops and sidings with plenty of wagons. The houses across back in Astley Street are in fact the other side of not only the River Tame valley, but also the Peak Forest Canal and a L&NWR line. (B.K.B. Green)

East, around 1950. Working heavily, probably as a result of a signal check, is a fitted freight passing the junction, from the left. The nearby Brookside sidings, loops and line to Stalybridge tended to swamp the local goods facilities here. Heading towards Manchester along the down goods is J39 class 0-6-0 No 64712. Meanwhile, passing under our feet is another goods train on the up main line with tarpaulin covering the contents of the open wagons. (E. Oldham Coltas Trust)

East of Guide Bridge

Up fast train, leaving Ashton Junction, Dukinfield, 1933. D11 class 4-4-0 No 5505 *Ypres* gets its train underway after its Guide Bridge stop along the up main line, having just passed under the girder bridge. It is probably heading home as it was allocated to Neasden. In three years' time, at its visit to Gorton works, it received new cylinders and valves and outwardly its reversing arm had a curve in it; here it is straight. The colliery mentioned on the wagon to the right will be featured in a subsequent volume. All the signals facing us are for down trains. That on the left is for the main line, to its right. Trains, like the coal-carrying one on the right, could be held by the larger bracket. This controls movement along the down slow line with the choice of route onto the down main. The bracket on the extreme right is for trains on the down branch, from Stalybridge, who could proceed onto either of the down lines into the station. (Unknown)

Dukinfield, around 1949. About to pass under Astley Street bridge from the east is a stopping train, probably from Hayfield or Macclesfield. C13 class 4-4-2T No 67426 has just emerged from Gorton works after a general overhaul, complete with BR number and new owner's name on the side tanks. It never strayed far from Gorton being built there, at this time called the shed there 'home' and after half a century of service was scrapped there too. (H.C. Casserley)

Dog Lane, Dukinfield, 1914. A station in Dukinfield opened with the line on 17 November 1841, closing when the line to Stalybridge opened on 23 December 1845. A second station with the same name, Dog Lane, opened on 1 May 1846; economy measures resulted in it closing from 1 November the next year. Across the main lines are Dewsnap sidings, with several wagons in them, the train obscuring the controlling signal box and much of the imposing gantry. Having recently been completed by the adjacent wagon works at Dukinfield, this collection of ambulance vehicles is setting off for Southampton. At the front is B2 class 4-6-0 No 428 *City of Liverpool*. (Unknown)

East Junction, 1949. Probably destined for Dewsnap sidings ahead, as it waits on the up main, is O2 class 2-8-0 No 63785. Having been coaled at Gorton, it is ready for a trip east across the Pennines. To the rear of the engine are the pair of lines from the up/down goods lines curving north towards the Stalybridge branch and connections to Yorkshire, dating from 1907. In the background are the shunters' mess rooms at Brookside. The wonderful set of signals are indicating it is to pass onto up goods No 2 at the point work just in-front of it. The right-hand arm would be for companion goods line No 3 whereas the tall post is for No 1. Transfers to the up main would be sanctioned by the arm on the left. (H.C. Casserley)

Guide Bridge East, 1969. Over-seeing events is the small, 36-lever, wooden signal box, complete with associated corrugated iron sheds. The magnificent lattice bracket signal controls train movements along the goods lines. This well-maintained wooden box had recently been painted. On the left is the wooden facilities shed for the signal men and next to it a sleeper-built coal bunker. (M.A. King)

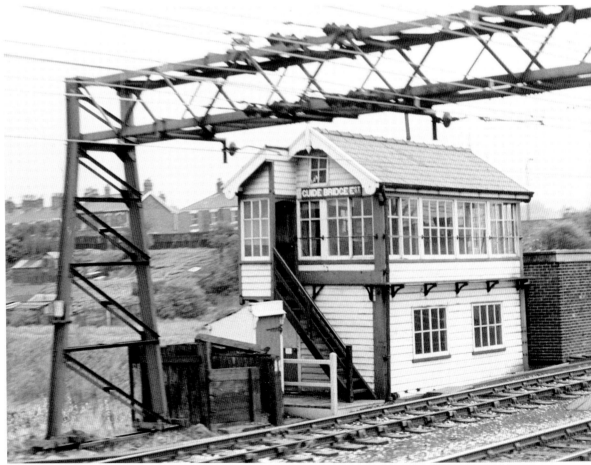

Dukinfield, 1901. Odd as it seems to us today, but several areas to the east of Manchester had coal mines. Dewsnap Pit and Astley Deep Pit were owned by Francis Dukinfield Astley; it operated as Dunkirk Coal Company. This company had a coal yard adjacent to Ardwick station. At the opening of Astley Deep Pit in the late 1860s, a hundred years of production was promised. It was, at that time, the deepest pit in the country and tapped into the 'Lancashire Black Mine' seam. It had taken 12 years to reach and cost £100,000. A second seam, 'Dukinfield Marine Band', was mined. This coal burned fiercely giving high temperature and so was widely sought after for steam engines, mills and railway engines, it was around 10 per cent dearer than other coals. Around 400 people worked here, 24 hours a day extracting up to 500 tons per day. Dewsnap Pit employed slightly less; both employed well over 100 men each above ground, However, disasters of 1870 and of 1874, in which 54 men died, the youngest was only 10 years old, meant a slowdown in production leading to eventual closure in 1901. A blue plaque, erected in 2001, in a turning grass and wooded turning circle at the end of at Woodbury Crescent, remembers the incident. What a contrast from the site it commemorates. In this map extract, from three years prior to closure, it can be seen that Dewsnap sidings had a previous name and were still in their infancy. The carriage works are still at least ten years away. (Crown Copyright, Tameside Library Archives)

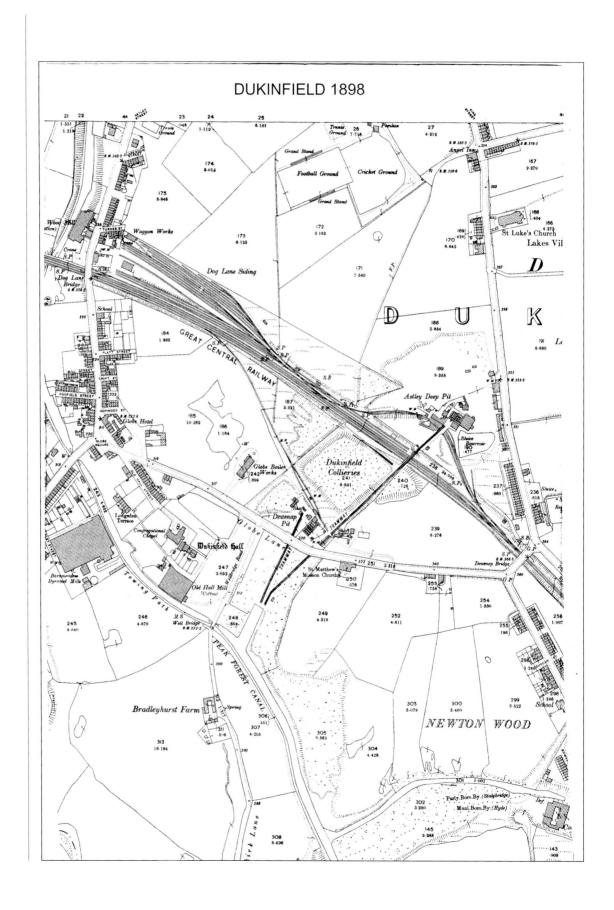

DUKINFIELD 1898

DUKINFIELD 1916

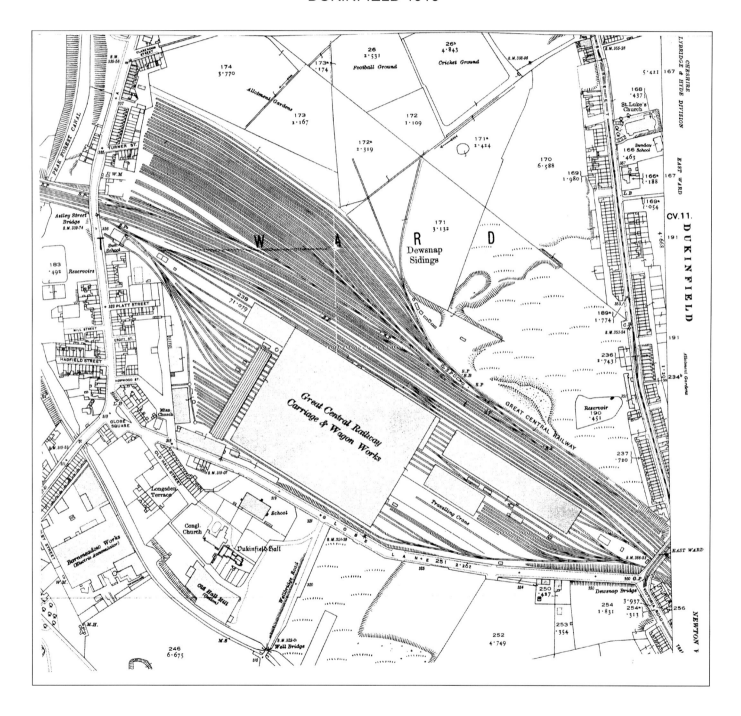

Dukinfield Carriage & Wagon works

The construction and maintenance of both locomotives and carriages & wagons initially was carried out at Gorton. However, being in a built-up area, there was little room to expand as business dictated. Therefore, in the early 1900s, the decision was taken by the GCR directors to expand the locomotive section by finding a new place for the carriage & wagon side of its operations. A 29½ acre site was found across the main running lines from Dewsnap sidings, on land formerly occupied by Dewsnap Colliery. The access lines and buildings were opened around 1910 and being new, the opportunity to operate with the best up to date machinery was taken, producing a modern and well-equipped set of workshops. They employed 1,400 men and *a number of girls* illustrating the changing role of women in society. Consisting mainly of one large brick building, it had its workers' access on Globe Street and wagons were usually received/dispatched at the eastern end and supplies at the other end. (*Crown Copyright*)

Dukinfield product, 1933. While this picture shows 4-4-2T Class C13 No 5009 in all its glory, it also shows two new clerestory coaches outside the works. At the western end of the main building is a traverser so that completed units can be moved onto lines and so be hauled away by engines. (GCRS)

Opposite: **Carriage construction, 1920.** The largest building is organised into many parallel lines with a wide gangway between. This enabled an elevated platform to be built between the lines from which the workmen could apply their trades. On the right, it appears to have a device at the level of the buffers. In 1915, Robinson, the CME of the GCR first fitted his anti-collision buffers and interlocking fenders to coaches. Both were designed to minimise problems in the event of an accident. The former improved the cushion effect of buffers while the latter were intended to keep the coaches from moving laterally and to prevent telescoping in the advent of an accident. While increasing the weight of a coach by 2 tons their usefulness was never tested, thankfully.

Dukinfield products, mid 1950s

(Pictures from *H.C. Casserley* and notes from *J. Quick*)

This non-corridor, 7 compartment Brake 3rd E5863E (at Peterborough) was 60ft long. Many such vehicles were built, during 1912-13 to GCR diagram 3A9, for suburban passenger work.

Giving service for almost 45 years was this 60ft kitchen car, at Cambridge, Originally No E5127E was built in 1914 as a composite restaurant car to diagram 5M2. It was rebuilt to this kitchen car in 1935, also at Dukinfield to diagram 5G4 in BR carmine and cream livery. (Ex-RC No 35)

Dukinfield products, late 1950s

Over the duration of the Grouping (1923-47,) the number of passengers carried on the LNER had fallen by over a third and the number of coaches by a fifth. From 1932, the company trialled a different method of wagon frame construction at its Dukinfield works. This was based on the part riveting and part welding with the resultant frame being lighter. In the mid-1930s, the LNER found it had over-capacity in building new wagons. Consequently, it decided to concentrate this activity at York and Darlington leaving a reduced workforce at Dukinfield to repair vehicles.

Dukinfield, 1948. Due to a shortage of space at Gorton, engines destined for scrap were stored between the buildings and the main lines. It is hard to believe that C4 class 4-4-2 No 262, built in 1906 would haul the company's crack express trains and would end its days like this. The brickwork of the building's walls was painted in khaki/brown during the Second World War to confuse the enemy aircraft as to their position. (H.C. Casserley)

The GC 10T coal wagon with grease axle boxes is typical of the sort repaired here, seen at Wellingborough. The works built new vehicles and repaired around 3,000 vehicles per year. They were not only for the GCR but also for other companies including ones they were partners in such as the CLR and the MSJ&AR as well as competitors, like the GER. (Guy Hemmingway and H.C. Casserley)

3-plank wagon, no date. Built for the Civil Engineer's Department, this wagon was returned to the mass of sidings east of Guide Bridge in between tasks. Note the covers over the axle boxes. (BPC)

Opposite above: **Cylinder wagon, 1938.** All railway companies lit their early coaches with gas; at the Grouping, the LNER had about 12,000 gas-lit vehicles. As time progressed, many were converted from flame burners to electricity, by 1928 roughly a third were illuminated by this new method. It was at Ardwick, as well as Sheffield and Cleethorpes, that cylinders were refilled. At Ardwick carriage sidings, and nine other places on the ex-GC system, the reservoirs on coaches were filled from tank wagons. This double cylinder wagon has just received its six-wheel underframe from a retired GCR coach. Such wagons were introduced by the MS&LR in 1892. Six were built at Dukinfield in 1933, two had three cylinders, the others, a single 6ft diameter cylinder. The last were not withdrawn until the BR era. (Unknown)

Dewsnap sidings

East of the Peak Forest Canal and the adjacent River Tame was home to collieries over the years, for example Astley Deep Pit. When they became exhausted the land was commandeered by the Great Central Railway from around 1901 and many blind ending sidings were laid out. Their role was to sort out wagons, many emanating from Liverpool's Brunswick and Huskisson yards, arriving via the Manchester Central Station Line and so avoiding passage across central Manchester, as well as empty wagons arriving from the businesses and industries served by the company, mostly to the east of Manchester. Growth of traffic meant that the number of sidings was expanded to reach fifty-six at its zenith. However, pictures of the complex are rare; it wasn't accessible and so occasional glimpses from passing trains are as good as it gets.

Bringing/removing wagons to the yard

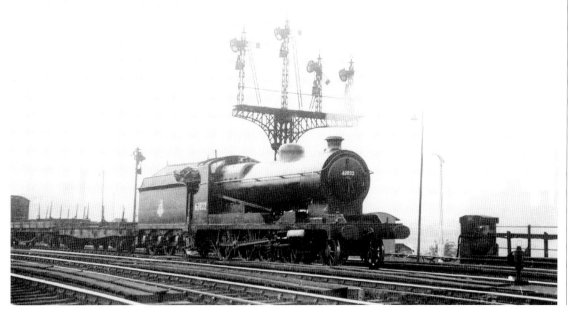

Reception lines, 1950. Having passed through Stalybridge, where it forms the county boundary, the River Tame is crossed by the main line before it meanders its way south to Stockport. There it meets the River Goyt and the Mersey is born. The original stone bridge was widened when the lines were quadrupled. One hundred yards east and the Peak Forest Canal is passed over which, as seen here; O4 class 2-8-0 No 63822, of 1918 vintage, is crossing, probably to enter one of three reception roads. (H.C. Casserley)

Down goods, 1950.
The footplate crew are taking a relaxed view of life as they probably wait a pathway around the curve to Guide Bridge North and onto Stalybridge. Ageing 'Pom-Pom' LNER J11 0-6-0 No 4368 on a local freight trip hides siding full of wagons. Notice the E added to above the number indicating the region of origin ready for the BR re-numbering. The sidings look full.
(H.C. Casserley)

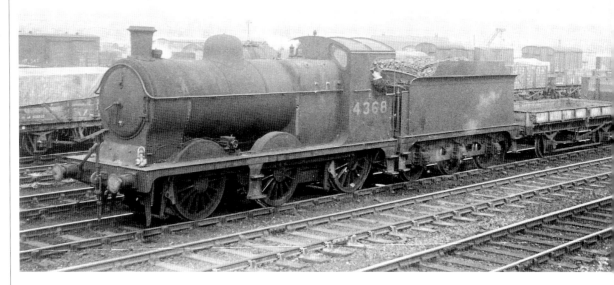

Dewsnap sidings, 1950. Conceived in a hurry during the Second World War, these engines were of the simplest design. They were meant to be heavy goods engines, built to help us win the war and little thought was given to the subsequent fate of these 'throw away' engines. The War Department allocated this engine the number 77021 after its construction by the NBL in 1943. It saw service on the Netherlands Railways, which, incidentally, saw these engines as a stop-gap prior to complete electrification, before returning to be allocated No 3002 by the LNER at New England shed, from 1945. Here it is line with other engines, probably after receiving its BR number-economy style! (H.C. Casserley)

How Dewsnap yard worked

Dewsnap was a focal point for goods traffic until, in 1935, Mottram yard was built and then became the principal point for sorting up trains, Mottram, some five miles away, the down wagons. The map on page 83 may help. There are several reception lines between the quadruple running lines and the signal box. No 1 could hold 70 wagons, smaller No 2 Reception line (53 wagons). Next follows No 3 Reception (55 wagons) and finally, a much smaller sidings, holding only 35 wagons sidings used for trips to/from Ashburys. Trains would arrive and halt near the signal box. There, the hauling engine would be detached and replaced by a tank engine or diesel shunter in later days. Shunting engines would haul a train from the reception lines into one of the five shunting necks, to the right. From there the train would be pushed back into one of the, eventually, 57 blind sidings, being sorted as this went on; there was no hump to assist sorting, although the far ends of the sidings were on a rising gradient to stop them hitting the stop blocks too fast. The sidings capacity was 2,431 wagons. The method was rather crude, but effective. After the wagons had been separated, 'Chaser' pursued the 'cut' and applied their brakes; too late and you had a long walk back, too soon and the next 'cut' would collide too forcefully, perhaps causing a derailment. In this manner trains for up destinations were assembled.

Dewsnap sidings, around 1910. The 40 levers in the signal box here didn't control movements along the main lines, only the up/down goods and their connections to the sidings. These sidings, along with others nearby, use to be the main sorting sidings for wagons along the main line to/from the Sheffield area. Posing are a selection of staff, mostly 'Chasers', with their wooden poles for attaching/detaching wagons. Not allowed to leave his cabin, but wanting to be in the picture, is the signalman. (BPC)

Prevention of accidents

In the late 1920s the 'Big Four' railway companies produced a joint booklet to encourage safety at work. To illustrate the seriousness of the problem, in its introduction it states, 'Every year between 200 and 300 railwaymen are KILLED, and in addition SEVERAL THOUSAND meet with accidents which lay them aside for days, weeks, months or for always.'

Obituary, 1906. The very nature of the jobs at Dewsnap, and other sorting sidings, means that they performed them in the dark, wet and with snow on the ground, additional hazards. The booklet also implores, 'Study the risk and the best ways of avoiding them', sounding much the same today. (Great Central Railway Journal)

The third man from the left, posing outside the signal box has a shunting pole. This, when used properly, enabled him to uncouple wagons, acting as a lever. With so many (young) men working here, risks will always be taken.

Foot caught through stepping on rail and slipping off. Many men have been trapped in this way.

Another great danger with such a work force is recognised in the booklet. Practical Jokes. 'In the excitement of playing practical jokes, men easily overlook the presence of danger. Many a prank, intended "just for fun," has resulted in a man losing a limb, his sight, or his life. The best way is not only to refrain from any such nonsense on railway premises, but also to make it a rule to discourage or prevent foolish play on the part of other.'

Dukinfield

Dewsnap Bridge, no date. Having just passed Dukinfield works, visible over the bridge, this push-pull unit heads along the up line towards Hyde Junction, possibly for Glossop. The fireman is looking out of the cab for the signals ahead. How marvellous it must have been as a youngster to have lived in one of the houses on Victoria Road, backing onto the line: trainspotting in all weathers!
(E. Oldham)

Dewsnap Bridge, no date. Having cleared all the junctions and the stop at Guide Bridge, an east-bound express prepares to tackle the ascent towards Woodhead, thirteen or so miles at about 1 in 117 gradient. B1 class 4-6-0 No 61162 (1947-65) will not find its lightweight train, possibly for Marylebone, much of a problem though. Contrastingly, ex-L&NWR trains to London would be frequently twice as long. (J. Suter Collection)

Hyde Junction, no date. Although not the best of pictures, it is included as it has some interesting details not seen on other views. J39 class 0-6-0 No 2691 heads along the main line, passing the signal box, on the left. Behind the box is a wonderful bracket signal for down trains. The post on the left, being the lowest as it is the least used, is for trains to access the carriage works. Next to it is an arm that would indicate to the driver that Down Goods No. 2 is his route whereas the post on the right would mean a trip to Down Goods No. 1 line. The tallest post would denote that the down main is the route it will be taking. On the extreme right is a siding, a link to this would enable coal wagons, as seen on the right in Victoria siding, supply the mill in the rear with fuel. In the late 1950s an O4 class 2-8-0 on the slow line emanating from Dewsnap sidings, failed to obey a signal and instead of stopping, carried on ploughing into the stone wall. (GCRS)

Hyde Junction, 1949. This picture is deceptive. The passengers make an interesting study. Possibly a daughter, complete with hat and gloves, has come to meet her parents. The father, complete with cigarette, carries a small suitcase and walks ahead of the two women, and possibly a child. Note the practise of etching a station's name onto the glass for the gas lights. Daniel Adamson's engineering works are the buildings in the background. The illusion is that the passengers, station and train are all connected somehow, but they are not. There were only platforms on the Joint Line towards Hyde and the train is on a different pair of tracks of the main line. On its way to Glossop and Hadfield is very recently re-numbered C14 class 4-4-2T No 67449. The extra coal and water carrying capacity of this class compared to C13s is hard to spot. The signals are for the down main line and show that at Hyde Junction, there are pairs of lines heading west. (W. Camwell, The Stephenson Photographic Collection)

Hyde Junction, 1948. East of Dewsnap and the line threads its way through Hyde and is surrounded by mills and engineering factories. While the main line turns east, a joint MS&LR/MR line branches off south towards Marple. Passenger stations in this area were on the branch, on the left are the station buildings on the down platform at Hyde North (ex-Hyde Junction) station with a lamp and a warning notice making an appearance, as well as a down signal, both partially obscured by the trees. Facing us is a down lattice bracket signal; ahead and the lines are quadruple all the way to Ardwick – fast on the left and slow on the right. Eyeing us up with suspicion is a member of the footplate crew of J11 class 0-6-0 No 4435 of Gorton shed, as he takes his stopping train towards Newton station. On the right are the premises of Hyde Junction Iron Works. (Unknown)

Newton (for Hyde), ('Newton F'ied' - you have to say it quickly!) **external view. 1984.** Although an important district, Hyde never had a station on the main line and had to share with Newton. The passenger station is accessed, rightly, from a small lane off the Sheffield Road, just west of a nine-arch viaduct. Appropriately, at the other end of the station the line passes under a bridge on which several roads meet, including Ashton Road, all as it should be for a station that opened with this section of the line on 17 November 1841, 2½ miles east of Hooley Hill. This view of the stone booking office is from that access lane, looking north. (N.D. Mundy and BPC)

Carvings, 2013. On the chimney, carved into stone, is the company's logo; the date when these buildings were erected is on the end wall, (1883). (BPC)

Newton entrance, 2013. Painted in the colours of its new operators (Northern Rail) is the woodwork surrounding the entrance and the roof supports. This makes up for the hidden aspect of the station and its poor access. (BPC)

Newton (for Hyde), internal views. Passengers have to climb steps to get onto the down platform and through a subway too for services to the south, arriving through this blackened stone doorway. A little further along the platform is this well built, sizeable shelter for Glossop-bound passengers. Manchester-bound passengers have the benefit of a substantial brick shelter, the back of which can be seen in the external view. (Great Central Railway Society)

Wartime pictures

While wartime pictures are rare, those from signal boxes are extremely rare. Few people had cameras in those days and taking an interest in railways was viewed with suspicion and taking pictures meant that you were up to no good, access to a signal box was almost treated like sabotage. In fact, soldiers guarded important places like Woodhead tunnel entrances and Godley Junction. The War Office issued a ban on railway photography. We are indebted to Eric Oldham for taking such pictures, some taken during his 'Games' lessons as the field of Hyde Grammar School backed onto the line.

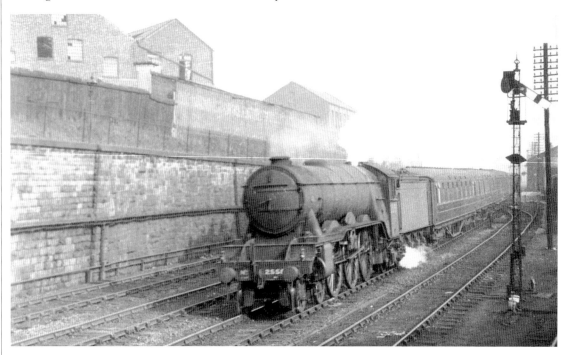

Above: **Newton (for Hyde), 1942.** Newton station is on a slight concave curve. Racing north is an express from Marylebone in the capital, to London Road, Manchester having been given the road by the company lattice lower quadrant semaphore signal. Given the conditions, smartly turned out A1 Pacific No 2558 *Tracey*, later re-numbered to 60059, hauls the train around the curve passed the high retaining wall on the left. Its original high sided tender has been replaced by an old GN type with a coal rail on the top to increase the coal capacity. On the right is the goods shed, this view having been taken from the signal box.

Opposite above: **Newton, 1942.** Heading towards Manchester is a down freight with LNER 4-6-0 class B5 No 5183 in charge. This class of engines, 'Fish Engines', were built with 6ft 1in driving wheels and expected to work the important Grimsby to Manchester (as well as other destinations) fish trains at express speed. Such trains would run into the exchange sidings at Ashton Moss for splitting up and distribution. It is estimated that around the turn of the twentieth century, Grimsby was handling a quarter of all rail-borne fish in the country, passing over 80,000 tons annually to other carriers just for London. The shift from rail to road started after the Great War and took until the mid-1970s before the practise was discontinued by rail.

Opposite below: **Streamlined engine.** About to pass under Victoria Street, adjacent to the signal box, on the left, is A4 Pacific No 4495. *Golden Fleece* in blue livery in April 1941. Although not common, A4 Pacific engines did make several visits to the Manchester area. Other wartime visitors were Nos 4488 *Union of South Africa*, 2512 *Silver Fox* and 4467 *Wild Swan*, all visited Gorton at some time. A Royal Train from London Road to Sheffield was hauled by 4466 *Sir Ralph Wedgwood* on 8 March 1945. Most famous of course, is No 4498 *Sir Nigel Gresley* in late February 1938 as part of a publicity tour for the Flying Scotsman train working to Manchester Central station.

Newton station.
A push-pull set, with the engine, typically a C class 4-4-2T, at the rear, is just about to stop at the station, en route to Glossop, the engine is C13 No 5193. Quite when this style of service was introduced is unclear, but it was in this decade. Notice the load gauge over the down loop. On the up-side, shunting is taking place with private owner's wagons much in evidence. The workman is carrying a shunter's pole. By placing this on a buffer, engaging the three-link coupling and pressing down on the other end the 1st order lever principle will enable him to uncouple wagons simply.

Godley, no date.
This view is down Mottram Road, east, to its junction with Station Road, from the right. On the left, Sheffield Road joins. The undulating nature of the terrain necessitated a cutting and here a short viaduct. Through the arches can be seen a factory. Initially margarine it later made ice cream with its owner' name, Walls, proudly proclaimed on the wall. (John Ryan Collection)

Leaving Godley, 1920s. Having passed through the station, an express for Manchester is getting into its stride. Recently built at Gorton D11 this 'Improved Director,' 4-4-0 No 510 *Princess Mary* called Neasden 'home' at this time. It received its BR number, 62664 in 1948, remarkably lasting until 1960. (GCRS)

Godley junction & station. With the original station having closed in 1842, a year after opening, Godley had no station for the next 24 years. This one, opening on 1 February 1866, coincided with the branch from the main line to Woodley arriving and was a short distance east of the original. The main line to Manchester is sweeping through, curving to the right. On the left is the Cheshire Lines route to Woodley, Stockport and eventually, Liverpool. Accessed from Station Road are the main station buildings in the 'V' so created with there being separate provision for the two different railway company employees. Connecting the two MS&LR platforms is a handsome covered footbridge; on the CLR side there was no such luxury, with passengers having to walk across the tracks. The reality was that with few passenger trains probably most stopped opposite the buildings and the island platform being rarely used. Appearing above the second engine is the signal box, a 1916 replacement for an earlier, probably 1880, one. (BPC)

Main line trains. 1952. Taken from towards the end of the Manchester platform and an up-freight train is captured. Trying to keep a good head of steam, and speed, is a fitted freight train with O4 class 2-8-0 No 63577 is at the helm. The steelwork awaits the overhead wires. Note the lamp at the top of the stairs on the footbridge. (Jim Davenport)

1939. Crossing the point work that leads to the Cheshire Lines route, as overseen by the 44 lever signal box on the left, is LNER class B7 4-6-0 No 5037 with a down goods train. The signal box is now at the end of the up platform, a position it took up from 1916. (C.A. Appleton)

Local train, October 1953. Life is not all about flash express trains tearing through stations. It is also about slow moving freight trains and humble stopping passenger trains such as this. In the final months of steam haulage, Gorton's class J11 0-6-0 No 64413 restarts its train for Glossop. This is one of around 20 such trains stopping here on weekdays, taking around 25 minutes from London Road. Electrification, from June the next year, would double the frequency and reduce the time to only 18 minutes. (N. Harrop)

Godley, up shelter. Surrounded by lines is the up platform with this basic provision for passengers. They would have waited in the station buildings on the other platform and only wandered across to the up platform when the train was due. The shelter isn't at the base of the footbridge's steps and so passengers wanting comfort had to walk along the platform. (GCRS)

Opposite above: **Buildings at Godley, 1988.** The LNER built a signal engineers' depot at Godley (the stone building in the background), opposite the Walls' building (the brick building on the right). Pre-Second World War and the company had a control office in one of the offices at London Road station. However, with the possibility of bombing during the war, a safer location was sought. The single storey stone building, complete with steel shutters for the windows and concrete roof, was built here. While incapable of withstanding a direct hit, the walls, roof and windows were 'blast proof'. With their area spreading from London Road probably as far as the tunnel mouth and someway along the Cheshire Lines route, this was seen as a prudent move to protect such a vital part of the rail network. The area didn't escape enemy activity; a bomb landed along the branch, not far from the turntable along the line to Woodley, but apart from a crater, did little damage. (J. Lloyd)

Opposite below: **Godley Junction signal box, exterior 1972.** This 44-lever wooden cabin box is viewed from a Manchester bound train, it being at the end of the up platform. (M. A. King)

Cheshire Lines branch

Godley, 1935. At almost 11.30am, one of the company's crack express trains obeys the 25mph speed limit as it passes from the main line to Cheshire Lines metals. C1 class Atlantic 4-4-2 No 3276 passes on the branch from Godley to Woodley. It will have started at 8.55am in Hull Paragon and, after an engine change at Sheffield, is soon to reach Stockport Tiviot Dale. Afterwards it will travel via Skelton Junction and at Glazebrook, will reach the main line for Liverpool Central. This rather roundabout route was taken to avoid a reversal in Manchester Central. This line was extensively used by coal trains for Liverpool's docks and for the Aintree race meetings, especially the Grand National. A later train, the 2.50pm from Hull followed the same route. However, it stopped here (at 5.29pm) for the detachment of its two rear coaches, the front of the train proceeded to Liverpool Central. Waiting in the down main platform would be a light engine. The two coaches were then pulled back onto the main lines and pushed up to this waiting engine by a local shunting engine. This train now went forward to Manchester London Road (arriving at 5.57pm), stopping at Guide Bridge only. Sometimes this turn was given to engines running in after servicing at Gorton. As an added complication, the engine taking this shuttle would leave Gorton at 4.08pm. Consequently, on the sprint into London Road it would be travelling tender first. This was to ensure that its next turn, the 6.31pm to Sheffield, it was facing the right way round. (Unknown)

Aintree race special, 1935. Although a poor picture, it is included for interest value. Replenishing the water supply in its tender is B3 class 4-6-0 No 6165 *Valour* of Immingham shed, coupled next to D9 class 4-4-0 No 6030, of New Holland shed. The coaches originated in Cleethorpes and Skegness; two engines were needed ensure the train kept to time, especially through the Woodhead tunnel, destination Aintree for the race meeting. Passengers are taking advantage of this stop to stretch their legs on the island platform. A water tank, on the left, supplying not only this water column but one at the up end of the branch platform at which returning trains from race meetings at Aintree would stop to replenish their water supplies. A steady procession, but rarely pictured, of trains passing through Godley, around 6pm, must have been a stirring sight. Pre-war, it wasn't uncommon for station staff to ask kitchen car attendants to place their bets and upon the return trip, hopefully, deliver their winnings. (English Heritage. NMR)

Godley station name boards, date unknown. In the apex of the 'V' of its platforms there was a board reading:

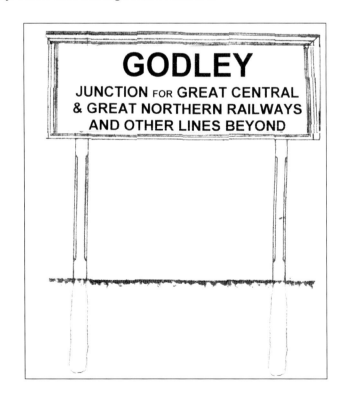

While both railways mentioned were part of the Cheshire Lines Railway there was also a third partner, the Midland Railway. Therefore, its omission is strange. Perhaps at that time only those railways mentioned ran trains to Godley with the MR having no services to the station.

At one time a board on the up platform read,

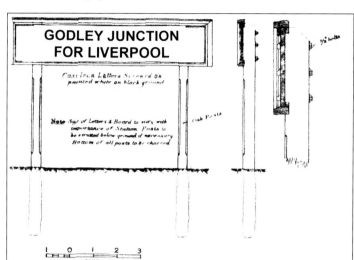

Beyond Godley

Skelton Junction, 1939. The rear coaches will be just passing the signal box that controls the branching off from the main line to Glazebrook of this 600yd curve. A speed limit of 30mph is in force and the train will shortly pass under the Glazebrook line (and the Broadheath link too) before meeting the MSJ&AR line at Deansgate Junction. The signalman in that box has pulled lever no. 1 to lower the signal on the tall post, on the left, with an interesting finial. The driver of K3 class 2-6-0 No 2396 is keeping a close eye on events as he controls his train down the gradient. Ahead is Altrincham station and then, still on Cheshire Lines, to Chester. This train is a special, hence the number '2' on the front, for Chester races; the winner of the last Chester cup until 1945, was *Winnebar*. (CM & JM Bentley)

Glazebrook, 1939. This train is carrying the Directors of the L&NER to the last Easter meeting at Aintree, Liverpool, before war broke out. Grand National day was at that time on a Friday; it is only in post war times that it has moved to a Saturday. Due to the large number of special trains to Aintree, each was given a special number, seen here affixed to the hand rail at the front. *CLC* refers to Cheshire Lines Committee (a joint Midland, Great Northern and MS&LR venture). While the origin of this long train is most probably London, Marylebone, it was pictured in Sheffield Victoria. The immaculately turned out engines are pilot B3 class (ex-GCR class 9P) 4-6-0 No 6165 *Valour* and B2 class 4-6-0 No 5424 *City of Lincoln*: double heading over the Woodhead route would have been necessary if the passengers weren't to miss the first race! Having left the ex-MS&LR main line at Godley, it has just joined the main Manchester to Liverpool CLR main line – witness the tall bracket junction signal in the rear – here at Glazebrook. (W. Potter)

LINE TO STALYBRIDGE

Trains have been using this route since its opening on 23 December 1845 and today it is the main line route for cross Pennine express services between Manchester and Leeds. Indeed, if the directors of the original company, the Sheffield, Ashton-under-Lyne & Manchester Railway had had their way, then this would always have been the case. Despite several of them also being directors of the Huddersfield & Manchester Railway, they were unable to persuade the latter company to link up with their line at Stalybridge and not to the line that was later absorbed by the L&Y. Subsequently, L&NWR trains from Leeds went to Victoria station and then to Liverpool rather than the SA&MR London Road terminus. In 1842, soon after the opening of the main line station at Ashton & Hooley Hill, the railway company encouraged the development of a bus service, horse drawn, linking Stalybridge and Ashton with the arrival/departure times of main line trains.

Guide Bridge, 1951. Looking east from the footbridge shows C13 class 4-4-2 No 67401 emerging from one of the numerous lines in between sidings full of wagons pulling interesting coaches into the station. The train's Permission to Proceed onto the main line would have been granted by the signalman in Ashton Junction box, behind and to the right, pulling a lever to allow the lower arm, on the signal post by the second coach, to fall. Aren't those lamps cute? They indicate that the sidings were so well used that some form of illumination was necessary. Note the wonderful signal gantry, and Guide Bridge North signal box, in the background, protecting that junction. Closer, and so more detailed, pictures of the signalling structure have proven impossible to find. (T. Lewis)

Above: **Guide Bridge, 1951.** Heading east along the up goods line is J11 class 0-6-0 No 64421 as seen from the footbridge. As the solid looking bracket signal ahead shows, its route is to the left along the line to Stalybridge. The engine's attempt to gather speed has unfortunately produced some obscuring smoke however, it is possible to pick out many full sidings containing a variety of wagons including loaded coal and a shunting engine in amongst them. (Raymond McCarthy)

Opposite above: **Guide Bridge, 1949.** While a good picture of the engine, unfortunately, the steel structure obscures some of the sidings, including the signal gantry, in this north east view. A wide variety of wagons and loads are shown, including a tarpaulin sheet that would have been used to put over a load in a covered wagon to protect the contents from the elements. Ex-LNER, now under new ownership, C13 class No 67422, allocated to nearby Gorton shed, performs the tasks; note the lack of high visibility clothing on the shunter. Between the sidings and the Birch Street Mills is the Manchester & Ashton-under-Lyne canal which started off adjacent to London Road Station in central Manchester. The MS&LR earned a reputation for being tardy and reluctant to spend money. Not only was this the cause of the L&Y leaving the tri-partite station at Stalybridge in 1869 but also in the next year at Guide Bridge there were differences. This time it was with the L&NWR. While both had agreed to share the cost of a new station for £10,000, it was the MS&LR that caused delays, resulting in the offer being withdrawn. Thus the company had to go it alone, resulting in station improvements (July, costing £4,510) 1874 and sidings alongside the Stalybridge line (October, costing £7,169). (John Lees)

Opposite below: **Workers at play, 1908.** Football was, and still is the No 1 recreation for young working-class men. Here we see a match between the many guards and shunters employed in the numerous sidings locally. There seems to be an imbalance between the sides, unless some of the spectators have joined in the team picture. There was a football ground now occupied by the buildings and fields of Poplar Street school, just south of Guide Bridge station near the Stamford Picture Theatre complete with a pub across the road – essential! (BPC)

GRAND FOOTBALL MATCH
GUARDS-V-SHUNTERS
GUIDE BRIDGE RAILWAY

Above: **Guide Bridge North, 1951.** Not only was this the meeting place for the lines from the main lines to create a triangle but also for the departure of a pair of goods lines, so congested was the area. This pair can be seen diverging to the left almost in front of the engine. Grosvenor cotton mill forms the background. Heading along the down main line is a train from Stalybridge, with Stanier 2-6-4T No 42542 easily handling the three coaches. On the right is the Down Goods line, passing around the back of the signal box we are in, linking to the main lines at East Junction. (Unknown)

Opposite above left: **Guide Bridge North Junction, 1974.** As Dewsnap sidings was just to the east of the Stalybridge line's north to west junction with the main line, then any trains destined for those sidings from the Stalybridge, and Yorkshire direction necessitated a reversal in the station. Hence, the company built a north to east curve from here to meet the main line almost on top of bridge No 26 as the line passes over the River Tame, opening in 1906. This view from a train passing along the up main line shows the departure east of the two lines that will curve to meet the main line at Guide Bridge East Junction. Here, and similarly at the other end of the curve, there is a down loop behind the 32-lever signal box. (M.A. King)

Opposite above right: **Guide Bridge North, 1971.** While the electrification scheme in the early 1950s replaced many signals with colour lights, it didn't, thankfully, remove them all. The line on the left is the down goods, some fifty yards before it passes behind the signal box to become the down loop. In the background can be made out the supports for the overhead wires along the curve to meet the main line at East Junction. Controlling movements along the down goods is this fine example of a GC lattice bracket signal. The arm on the shorter post would indicate that a train was to pass onto the down main line and proceed towards Guide Bridge station, meeting the main line at Ashton junction. Alternatively, and more often, the route would be to continue along the down goods, bypassing the pointwork at North Junction and turning east along the branch to East Junction. The two arms on one post refer to the point work by its base. These are Down sidings 1 & 2, the top arm being for the siding, No 2, on the left. (M.A. King)

Showing the reverse of the signals and the detail of the down sidings post better is this view slightly further south. The two lines in the background curve around to meet the down loop. Note the concrete lamp to make life easier for the shunting staff. (M.A. King)

Dukinfield Junction, 1953. The L&NWR built a line to avoid the congestion at Guide Bridge station. Their line from Denton Junction passed under the MS&LR main line and rose up to meet our line to Stalybridge, here just as ours crosses the River Tame. Later, an extension of the L&NWR line directly to Stalybridge station replaced this junction, making it only for the meeting of sidings, east and west of our line. The electrification programme also contained plans to energise the adjacent sidings, the overhead masts are up waiting the wires. A Class 5 engine is shunting using the main line under control of Dukinfield signal box with another engine similarly employed in the sidings. The concrete lamps seem a very fancy design for lighting up sidings. (C.H.A. Townley)

River Tame bridge, late 1950s. The River Tame passes under the SAMR main line east of Guide Bridge and has been on an enforced route parallel, to the east, of this branch line ever since. Here the river executes an 'S' bend, passing under the line, coming to lie next to it, on the west side. We are standing on the eastern bank as the river turns to go under the railway. Passing across the stone Stalybridge branch bridge is an unidentified LMS Stanier 2-6-0 heading north. Dukinfield Junction signal box is just getting into the picture on the left. Immediately in front of us is a steel girder bridge which carries the L&NWR lines from Denton Junction to Stalybridge. (C.T. Gifford)

Dukinfield station, exterior, around 1910. Once over the river and our line crosses the Peak Forest Canal, which the MS&LR bought in 1846. At opening on 23 December 1845, the station was a short distance further towards Stalybridge. This simply consisted of two platforms, with an open shed for passenger protection, approached by wooden steps. One of the nearby company cottages was used as a booking office and waiting room where the clerk-in-charge lived. In March 1863 the MS&LR agreed to re-build this rather miserable station, moving it 117 yards closer to Guide Bridge at a cost of £1,620. The line here is on a low viaduct and the station buildings were raised up by that amount. On the right is Wharf Street Tavern, with the substantial stone station buildings in the middle; access was via the stone steps. This is the down, to Guide Bridge, side. (Courtesy Stockport Library Archive)

Above: **Dukinfield station, interior, around 1920.** Having bought a ticket, the photographer has walked onto the opposite, up, platform. Note the extensive canopy between the two parts, reminiscent of those buildings on the Cheshire Lines Railway. Both platforms consisted of a central paved section flanked by timber extensions, this being adequate to cope with the normal short trains that stopped here. A train stopping here would be destined for Stalybridge and have the benefit of a stone building housing waiting and toilet facilities. (Courtesy Stockport Library Archive)

Opposite above: **Dukinfield, 1950.** Tea time catches the 5.30pm departure being pushed by Gorton based C13 class 4-4-2T No 67438 towards Stalybridge. While many such trains started from Guide Bridge, this was one of only two that originated from London Road, at 5.03pm. A same time departure from Victoria would get a passenger into Stalybridge fractionally earlier. BR adding the suffix, 'Central', in 1954 to distinguish their station from that of the ex-L&NWR rival a third of a mile north. (W.A. Camwell, The Stephenson Photographic Collection)

Opposite below: **Cavendish Street, 1932.** This road that passes almost north-south through Ashton under Lyne has a large number of bridges along its route. Immediately in-front of us is a girder bridge carrying the MS&LR line to Stalybridge, to our right. In the distance, near the horse and cart, the Manchester & Ashton under Lyne canal is crossed. The photographer is standing on a bridge over the River Tame with another girder bridge immediately behind carrying the L&NWR line, also to Stalybridge, over our heads. Interestingly, the border between Cheshire and Lancashire is on the bridge over the river, the differential road maintenance regimes are evident. Until 1902, there was a toll on this river bridge. (BPC)

Dukinfield Central (GCR) - 1

Above: **Ashton Arches, around 1960.** Carrying the line over King Street and subsequently over the Huddersfield Canal is an impressive stone viaduct. The River Tame doesn't pass through the arches but skirts their foundations. This was probably a contributory cause for several of these arches collapsing during construction on 19 April 1845 with the loss of 17 lives. The *Illustrated London News* carried a line drawing of the event. As the county boundary is the River Tame, some workers died in different counties resulting in compound inquests and grief for relatives. The replacement arches, seen here, were tested by driving an engine and coaches weighing a total of 84 tons over them. This, claimed the builder, represented the maximum weight the line would carry. Consequently, the inspector passed the line fit and it opened on 23 December 1845. The structure is still standing and in constant use today carrying the main line from Manchester to Leeds. (Eric Harrison)

Opposite above: **Timetable, 1922.** Note the gap for most of the working day when there were no trains, with minor additions on Saturdays. It also reveals that trains to Stalybridge worked the service back to Guide Bridge.

MANCHESTER, GUIDE BRIDGE, ASHTON, and STALYBRIDGE.—Great Central.

St. Michael's ... 9 ... 9 56 ... 11 2 ... 9 42 1049 1212 ... 7 55 ... 1025 ...
Liverpool (Central) ... arr. 8 15 9 10 8 45 9 22 9 30 10 3 ... 1015 ... 11 9 1125 ... 4 35 9 10 1056 1219 5 27 8 2 ... 1032 1050 ...

Up. — Week Days only.

Manchester (L.R.) dep. 6 57 0 7 35 8 0 ... 8 43 ... 1130 ... 1212 ... 1 10 5 10 4 20 ... 5 0 ... 5 40 ... 6 10 ... 8 5 ... 10 06 ...
Guide Bridge ... 6 26 7 20 7 46 8 20 ... 9 5 ... 1151 ... 1242 ... 1 40 5 47 4 40 ... 5 20 ... 5 59 ... 6 29 ... 8 23 ... 1019 ...
Dukinfield ... 6 29 7 23 7 49 8 23 ... 9 8 ... 1155 ... 1245 ... 1 43 5 50 4 43 ... 5 23 ... 6 3 ... 6 32 ... 8 31 ... 1022 ...
Ashton (Park Parade) ... 6 32 7 25 7 52 8 26 ... 9 21 ... 1159 ... 1247 ... 1 45 5 53 4 47 ... 5 26 ... 6 6 ... 6 35 ... 8 34 ... 1024 ...
Stalybridge 456 ... arr. 6 36 7 29 7 57 8 29 ... 9 15 ... 12 4 ... 1253 ... 1 48 5 56 4 51 ... 5 30 ... 6 10 ... 6 39 ... 8 38 ... 1028 ...

Down. — Week Days only.

Stalybridge ... dep. 5 5 ... 7 37 52 8 10 ... 8 45 ... 9 25 ... 1215 ... 1 27 ... 2 10 ... 4 10 5 10 5 42 ... 6 35 ...
Ashton (Park Parade) ... 5 9 ... 7 9 7 58 8 13 ... 8 48 ... 9 28 ... 1218 ... 1 30 ... 2 13 ... 4 13 5 13 5 45 ... 6 38 ...
Dukinfield ... 5 11 ... 7 12 8 1 8 15 ... 8 50 ... 9 30 ... 1220 ... 1 32 ... 2 16 ... 4 15 5 15 5 47 ... 6 44 ...
Guide Bridge 691 ... arr. 5 13 ... 7 14 8 3 8 17 ... 8 53 ... 9 32 ... 1222 ... 1 34 ... 2 19 ... 4 18 5 18 5 50 ... 6 48 ...
Manchester (L.R.) ... 5 41 ... 7 34 8 18 8 38 ... 9 15 ... 9 56 ... 1242 ... 2 13 ... 2 42 ... 4 37 5 45 6 30 ... 7 2 ...

H Central Station ; arrives London Road at 6 47 aft.   P Central Station ; arrives London Road at 10 10 mrn.

For **LOCAL TRAINS** and intermediate Stations between Manchester (London Road) and Guide Bridge, see page 703.
For **OTHER TRAINS** between Manchester and Ashton, see page 733; between Manchester and Stalybridge, see pages 456 and 549; between Dukinfield and Stalybridge, see page 456.

Ashton, Park Parade, exterior, 1964. Although arguably the most well-known, but not the most used, station in Ashton, it is remarkable that the only picture I have been able to unearth of its entrance is after its closure! Christmas came early in 1845 with this station opening on the 23 December. This large courtyard is formed where Park Parade and Warrington Street meet, the station being closer to the town centre than the company's other station in the town, (Central from 1954) which is only half a mile south. Passing through the two storey buildings led passengers into a train shed and onto the platform for Stalybridge. It was only from 30 July 1862 that the suffix 'Park Parade' was added to the station's name. The company's other station in the same town had to wait until nationalisation to be differentiated. Interestingly, the Joint station on the line to Oldham had boards that simply read 'Ashton'. (Kidderminster Railway Museum)

***Above*: Ashton-under-Lyne, no date.** We are probably standing right above the canal, at the end of the platform for Stalybridge; the Asda supermarket probably is in this place today. Access to the station was through the building on the left. The line and the station were actually built over the top of Lower Wharf Street which makes the solid appearance of the platforms interesting. The girders are reminiscent of the train shed once there. In the background, the goods yard seems busy with the signal box and signals behind them. Shunting was performed in the morning by an engine from Gorton which carried onto perform a similar act in the joint goods yard at Stalybridge. In the afternoon an engine from the L&NWR did the honours, in LMS days would have come from Newton Heath shed. (BPC)

***Opposite above*: Ashton warehouse, around 1910.** Adjacent to the passenger station was this substantial goods warehouse, the viaduct widening to meet it. The warehouses were accessed by both rail and canal. Road access was from Lower Wharf Street on the other side of the buildings. Some fifty feet below rail level, to the right of the viaduct, is the canal which passed into the right-hand building for unloading. Typical loads would have been cotton and coal. Officially this is a picture to record the dispatch of goods from the Jones sewing machine factory, adjacent to the L&NWR line in Hooley Hill. (Tameside Library Archive)

***Opposite below*: Approaching Stalybridge, 1956.** In January 1846, permission was given to double the line from Ashton to here. Turning east, the line crosses Whitelands and then heads for Stalybridge, just over a mile away, firstly in a cutting and latterly on an embankment. At one point, by Clarence Street and the three companies that converged on Stalybridge, all have their pair of tracks parallel to each other. Built by the MS&LR in 1893, this wooden signal box had 31 levers and the signalman would face onto the lines he controls with Bailey Street behind and below. This is the signal box, Stalybridge No1, that controlled the entrance to the joint (L&NWR/GC) goods yard and movements between these two company's pairs of lines, in both directions. To the east were three loops, which at their far end, were connected to the L&NWR lines which in turn were connected to the GC pair of lines. A signal box, 'Stalybridge No 1 Goods Junction' was sandwiched between the pairs of running lines. However, around 1909, the exit from the loops as well as the crossovers were removed together with No1 box enabling all the rest of the boxes in the area to be down numbered by one. So, although opening as 'Stalybridge No 2 Goods Junction', this box later became No 1. (Mike Christensen)

Views from Stalybridge No1 box, around 1960. Looking west, shows three discs at ground level. These controlled accesses to the loops called 'Mabholes sidings' after a number of adjacent dwellings. At street level is the appropriately named Boddingtons pub, The Pointsman. An Austerity 2-8-0 has just passed the box with a load of coal wagons. It will have passed around to the south of the station using the goods lines and at this point is switching from the L&NWR line to Stockport to the MS&LR line to Guide Bridge.
(Roy Harrison)

Above left: **MS&LR trains to Stalybridge, 1954.** A train on the MS&LR line from Guide Bridge is passing this fine GC bracket signal opposite Box No 1. These signals controlled the route ahead and the transfer of such trains onto the adjacent L&NWR lines. The latter then became the goods avoiding lines that by-pass the station to the south. Note the train on the left. It is passing west along the joint MS&LR/L&Y line that connected the two systems up dating from 1849 and after reaching L&Y metals, at Stalybridge Junction – the controlling box is trying to get into the picture – will be probably Manchester Exchange bound. (GCRS)

Above right: Looking east from the box shows the four lines coming from the station and No 2 box in the distance. To the left of the nearest bracket signal are the lines to Stockport (nearest) and Guide Bridge. Rising up diagonally to the left are the connecting lines to the L&Y system. The line immediately below us serves two loops, 'siding No 1 & No 2', which together with those at Mabholes served the goods yard, on the right. (Roy Harrison)

Left: This is Victoria Junction with the connection to the L&Y system off to the left. Protecting this junction from east bound trains is this magnificent signal gantry, built by the GCR. Most of the suburban trains ran into the two bays built as part of the 1880s rebuilding of the station, at the western end of the down platform. To enter the bays, trains obeyed the lower quadrant signals on the left and middle posts. The tallest post, with two arms on it, indicates the through line at the station. (GCRS)

About one hundred yards east, towards the station, and this bracket signal controlled the main line. The taller post is for the through line while the left-hand post is for the platform. Note the smaller 'calling on' arm on the main post. Its lowering, while the arms above were at 'stop' would enable another engine to come up behind a train already occupying the line, usually for banking purposes. The white diamond on the post indicates that this line is on a track circuit and so in the controlling signal box, no 2, there will be a light that will be illuminated when the line is occupied. This should prevent the signalman' forgetting' that there is a train still in that section and allowing another to enter it as well - with disastrous consequences. Rule 55 didn't apply, i.e. the driver doesn't have to inform the signalman of his presence. (GCRS)

Bay platforms

As part of the extensive rebuilding of the station in the 1880s these huge bays could accommodate up to nine coaches, sufficient for excursions, but many more than their humble trade warranted.

1956. Waiting in one of the bay platforms is C13 class 4-4-2T No 67417 with the 12.43pm (SO) to Guide Bridge. Note the scissors crossovers to allow engines to be released and so return the service. However, this train is 'rail motor' fitted and so can be driven from either end. It has only just arrived here being the 12.31pm (SO) from Guide Bridge, arriving at 12.39pm. (C.A. Appleton)

April 1948. However, in need of the engine release is this 5.27pm from Guide Bridge. N5 class 0-6-2T No E9343 has been uncoupled from the coaches, run around them and re-attached to them and is waiting departure at 5.45pm back to Guide Bridge. Nine minutes are allowed for this procedure. The prefix was added to the number the month before and would be converted into a '6' in February of the next year. Alterations to the platforms in 1858 resulted in a refreshment rooms being opened here from October the next year - they are still open and are an integral part of the 'Booze Trains' that are frequented on Saturdays along the L&NWR line to Huddersfield. (W.A. Camwell Stephenson Photographic Collection)

Above: 1948. Short local trips were often used to 'run in' new or locomotives which had been repaired at Gorton. Here, eight months old Class B1 4-6-0 No 1227 and still looking immaculate, pulls out some empty stock from the bay platform. At one of the main line platforms, a tank engine, No 77 from the other partner of the station, pauses. (W.A. Camwell Stephenson Photographic Collection)

Opposite above: GC connections, 1965. Unlike today's network, where there are few different routes between towns, in the 1960s there were alternative routes, always useful for excursion traffic. On the left is the massive bulk of the ex-L&Y goods warehouse and on the extreme right are the goods avoiding lines. Setting off from platform No 4 is B1 class No 61173. It will have originated at Castleford with its destination being the pleasure gardens and zoo at Belle Vue. As this is on the GC lines out from London Road station, this train will have to switch from one region to the other. Notice it is being cautiously signalled to proceed past No 2 box and thence onto GC metals by No 1 box and thence onto Guide Bridge and the GC system. This is the route taken by today's Trans-Pennine express trains; is history saying it was right and this was the route that really should have been favoured rather than passing onto the L&Y line or will the impending electrification prove us all wrong? (Coltas Trust)

Opposite below: Stalybridge, no date. The crossovers in the middle of the up/down platform lines enabled two trains of five coaches each to be handled at each. Hence tank engine, No1402, a 5ft 6in 2-4-2T with its train of L&NWR coaches occupying the eastern end of platform 3. In keeping with the joint station tradition is the signal box, once called 'Stalybridge station', no 3, of which spans the running lines. While the cabin is MS&LR, the frame, of 42 levers, is a G&SWR type. Access was by ladders from both platforms. Its role was the two sets of scissors crossovers between the through and platform lines as well as a trailing crossover between the up/down through lines (BPC)

Above: **Stalybridge, exterior, 1960.** The road we are looking across, Rassbottom Street, is on an incline, rising up to the right and passing under the railway on the left. When the joint station was enlarged, the main down platform and associated buildings were pushed from the lines, to the right. In the space created where the platform lines moved to the left to join with the through lines, an entrance was made. Through here and into the booking hall gives a passenger access to two ramps to the platforms; straight ahead for Huddersfield and Leeds, while turning left and passing in a subway for Manchester and Stockport. On the extreme right is the ex-L&Y station with a cobbled drive between the two stations. At the far end of this is a wall behind which, on the left, are the two bay platforms where passengers for Guide Bridge, Oldham, Manchester and Stockport would catch their trains. (BPC)

Opposite above: **John Summers Iron Works, 1950s.** The iron works was built adjacent to the canal before it crosses the River Tame in an aqueduct. With the coming of the railway Globe Iron Works decided to be connected to that system too. However, it was the other side of Bayley Street. Consequently, two small loops and a siding were provided in the joint goods yard, a branch from the latter crosses the road necessitating its closure to traffic. A Morris car is having to wait while 0-4-0ST *Mack* removes wagons from the works. The wagons behind the engine are in the sidings feeding the goods yard while those higher up are in No 2 siding, adjacent to the main line, the signals being just beyond the platforms. (Eric Harrison)

Opposite below: **Stalybridge, 1948.** Tempting as it is to think of Stalybridge as L&NWR/MS&LR territory, there was another partner, the L&Y, some of the time. A potted history of the station shows that while they weren't willing to be part of the expense of improving the station in the 1880s, the L&Y took their passenger services back to their own adjacent station they had left some years earlier. And so things were until the Great War. Economies forced the L&Y to the Joint station, their passenger station becoming subsumed into their goods undertakings, chiefly as a coal depot. Standing on the track serving the single platform looking east shows the remains of the passenger facilities. The often-pictured goods warehouse is on the left. The mineral wagons block some of the view of the cobbled lane up from Rassbottom Street, behind the buffer stop. On the right are the Joint station buildings with signals beyond them. (Stephenson Locomotive Society Photographic Collection)

Stalybridge, no date. Subsequent to the closure of its own passenger platform, the L&Y company ran its Victoria to Stalybridge service along its Ashton branch, the trains ending in the bays of the Joint station. Pictured around the Grouping, this 'Side tank' locomotive, No 18, looks spick-and-span as it awaits to depart back to Manchester. (John Ryan Collection)

MANCHESTER CENTRAL STATION LINE

As a partner in the Cheshire Lines Railway, the MS&LR found themselves unable to take advantage of this arrangement as much as they would like. This was because they, at London Road, were on the opposite side of the city from Central station, which they partially owned. While they could run trains to Liverpool using connections at Godley Junction, this necessitated the by-passing of Manchester which meant lost revenue. Also, the small, only eventually three platforms, at London Road restricted their ambitions. So, the company built this method of serving both cities with east to west coast trains. However, it had the disadvantage of necessitating a reversal in Manchester Central and the expense of another engine for the short distance to Liverpool. Originally, the line from Fairfield was to meet the CLR near Old Trafford, however, in the end it connected a couple of miles short of this at Chorlton. The gap, of Manchester South District Railway origin, was transferred to the CLR so MS&LR ownership ended at Chorlton Junction. Although the southern suburbs of Manchester were green, leafy and wealthy at that time, the early 1890s, experience should have told the Company that near big cities, only radial routes thrive and their peripheral one was unlikely to earn much money. However, with the construction of the Manchester Ship Canal (opening in 1894) then a 1906 link to it enabled the Company successfully to take full advantage of their links eastwards.

Overleaf above: **Midland Hotel, 1925.** With none of the major railways serving the city owning a quality hotel, the nettle was grasped by the Midland Railway to build a convenient, modern, luxury hotel for passengers wanting to stay over in Manchester. Built between 1897 and 1903 and costing £1.25m, this six-storey building looked, and was, expensive. It boasted air conditioning and several services within its confines such as, barbers, tailors, a chemist and a sub-post office which franked letters with a unique post-mark, 'Midland Hotel Manchester'. Most pictures of the building are of the front facing St. Peter's Square. We are standing in the station's forecourt looking at the rear of the hotel with the hotel's entrance, beneath the emblem, actually across the road (Windmill Street). The grand plan was to make the passage way, on the left, from station to hotel a prestigious affair, though, alas, it never happened. The building was not always favourably received, indeed, one commentator said, 'Although a good size for its purpose, but, the building, which attempts splendour, merely achieves vulgarity. It has size but no shape: its architectural decoration is meaningless: and, worst of all, it is built of an abominable combination of terracotta, glazed brick, and polished granite…. it receives its soot in a quiet unruffled way. Gradually the whole building becomes smooth and velvety…' (BPC)

Series 5007 - 4.   MIDLAND HOTEL MANCHESTER.   Davidson Brothers
                                                                                         LONDON

Manchester Central station

This is not meant to be exhaustive account of the station, as it was only jointly owned, so only a snapshot, from a MS&LR perspective, is explored.

***Opposite above*: External view, around 1895.** Although unfinished, the station opened for traffic on Thursday 1 July 1880. There is more than a passing resemblance to the MR's entrance to the capital in St Pancras station. The intention had been for a combined office block and station hotel in the forecourt. However, while the three owners, their names blazoned across the front, debated the design, wooden temporary structures were erected inside the train shed for tickets, waiting rooms and kiosks. Eventually, the MR built a hotel across the road to our right, facing not the station, but one of the city's prestigious squares. The temporary structures lasted the lifetime of the building as a station. Note the wide covered walkway linking the station and the hotel. (Courtesy of Manchester Libraries, Information & Archives, Manchester City Council m62730)

***Opposite below*: Circulating area, 1955.** Pictures of such areas are always wonderful opportunities to reflect on the social scene of the day. On the left is a bookstall with platform 6/5 behind it. Across the passage is a refreshment room with platforms 1 & 2 behind them. The small *Daily Mail* van is on the cab road to platform with platform 1 hard up against the brick wall, beyond the telegrams office. Behind us was a larger kitchen/dining/refreshment set of rooms with retail opportunities, toilets and waiting rooms to the right. With no raincoats in view and no big overcoats it is probably autumn or spring time when men rolled up their sleeves and women wore cotton dresses, albeit with a cardigan. Comments about the area suggested that the wooden buildings prevented 'circulation' and the booking office was more reminiscent of a seaside resort in December than that for a gateway to the capital, station. Statistics for 1959 show well over a million passengers booked arriving on 108 trains and departing on 98, on weekdays, with around 400 staff to assist. (Stations UK)

Internal view, 1965. The time is around 9am and an early morning train from Sheffield Midland (departing 7.03am) has just arrived. It will have stopped at all stations along the Hope Valley line, Stockport's Cheadle Heath then all stations to here. Canklow-based B1 class 4-6-0 No 61315 is waiting patiently while a tank engine backs in from the April sunshine to attach itself to the rear of the train. The coaches will probably be drawn out and parked in the numerous carriage sidings around the approaches to the station. This will allow the train engine to be turned and serviced before its next trip. Notice the engine release roads from the platforms. Interesting as these train and stock movements are, the real purpose of the picture is to marvel at the wonderful train shed. This consisted of 18 'ribs' which started off below platform level where they were bolted to masonry footings. These principal girders were 35ft apart and the absence of internal supports adds to the splendour of the building: the roof is 90ft above the anchor plates under the platforms. In the original plan there were three pairs of platforms such as these under the train shed. There was a wide space between platforms 2 and 3 to allow vehicle access. The brick walls at the sides are for enclosure and passenger protection, not support. The roof, walls and the glazed end panels really gave the sense of an enclosed space; however, they ruined the acoustics when trying to listen to announcements. (Gordon Coltas Trust)

Central station, 1960. What an exciting place was the station of my youth! There was always something happening, and the pervading smell of steam was ever-present. Looking from the end of platform 7, this picture shows the magnificent train shed with canopies extending from it giving passenger protection right to the ends of the platforms. Basically, the station as built, consisted of six platforms, in pairs with an engine release facility between each pair. This symmetry was spoilt when, on the right-hand side, an extra platform (8) was added in 1885, outside the curtain wall and this extended to create a seventh platform: with the diesel engine in it. A wooden extension to the side of platform 8, became platform 9, in 1905. In platform 3 is a tank engine, possibly on a sprint to Liverpool as part of the 'Punctual Service'. An express has just arrived at platform 5 and the empty carriages are about to be taken to the sidings by MR 0-6-0 No 44138. Having brought the express in, probably a class five tender engine, has been released from its coaches and now waits in the centre road awaiting, possibly, a pathway to Trafford Park shed for servicing. Note the trap point to prevent it straying onto either of the platform lines without permission. Two different styles of water column are in view, MR on the right. (P. Sunderland)

Platform 5, 1953. Having set off from Liverpool Central, this train would have passed the famous football ground and Throstle Nest East Junction, heading east, to arrive here. The train engine, at the other end of the platform, has been uncoupled from the front and this engine attached to what was the rear. D10 class 4-4-0 No 62658 *Prince George* of Trafford Park shed, is waiting for the allotted time, and then it will set off west, passing Throstle Nest East Junction, again, travelling west! However, this time it will turn south and head towards Chorlton Junction. Stops at Guide Bridge and Penistone would see the train arrive at Sheffield Victoria where a change of engine would probably take it via Doncaster to Hull. Electrification of the main line from London Road the next year would necessitate a change of motive power at Guide Bridge. Another such change, in reverse, at Sheffield Victoria will see steam attached finally for its trip east. (W.A. Brown)

Platform 9, 1948. German bombing in the Second World War rendered the Joint Line viaduct to Altrincham useless, just past Knott Mill station. However, the adjacent viaduct to here was unharmed. Lateral thinking by the railway officials enabled passengers from the Altrincham line to capitalise on the Cheshire Lines usage of Central by means of the junctions at Cornbrook. Electric trains ceased at Warwick Road and passengers changed to a steam shuttle service of three and another of four coaches which brought them into the city centre, here. Engines could use the middle track to be released from their coaches, here C12 4-4-2T No E7369 performs such a manoeuvre, although well after the viaduct was repaired. Tender engines then could use the adjacent turntable to prepare themselves for the return journey, of which there were 60/day. Attaching themselves to the front of the coaches a train would take Cheshire Lines metals until Cornbrook where it would then pass onto MSJ&AR lines to pass through to Warwick Road station. Note the number, built as No 1511 in 1899, becoming No 4511 after the Grouping, until the 1946 LNER renumbering when it carried No 7369. The E was a post Nationalisation idea which became the number '6' from 1/1949 (until demise in 1954) and shed (Trafford Park, 9/43 till 2/53) painted onto the front. This class were designed by Ivatt, of the Great Northern Railway and were slightly lighter, with one-inch larger driving wheels than the more common C13/14 classes. (H.C. Casserley)

Loco. servicing area, 1949. To the south of the approaches, high above street level was perched this rudimentary facility, if ever I saw an engine move near it when passing on a No 62 bus as a child, I always thought it was going to topple over! The turntable could accommodate 60ft engines/tender and was useful for turning engines that had worked from Liverpool or Trafford Park shed and needed turning. On turntable, complete with express train headlamps is B1 4-6-0 No 61313, note the lack of number on the smoke box door. There were three lines on which engines could be stabled, the ends of two occupying spaces under the water tank, the building in the left background. On the right are the supports for the gas holders at Gaythorn Street gas works, adjacent to the Oxford Road (MSJ&AR) line. (R.K. Blencowe Negative Archive)

Central station, 1954. With limited space for servicing carriages in the station, engines were needed to transport them to designated places. Having attached itself to the rear carriages of a train terminating at platform 6 at Central station, D10 class 4-4-0 No 62656 *Sir Clement Royds* heads for the carriage sidings at Cornbrook. (B.K.B. Green)

Central station, 1951. Meanwhile, heading in the opposite way, from carriage sidings to the platforms is aging J10 class 0-6-0 No 65148. (H.C. Casserley)

Shunting engine, 1951. Busying itself shunting outside Manchester Central station is ex-GNR class J69 0-6-0 No 68598. A small contingent of such engines called Trafford Park 'home' just prior to Nationalisation. This railway company was the original partner, with the MS&LR in the Cheshire Lines Railway, prior to the MR joining them. Such engines will have shunted the company warehouse adjacent to the passenger station, as well as most probably, other duties in the goods yard and carriage sidings at Cornbrook, for a price. (H.C. Casserley)

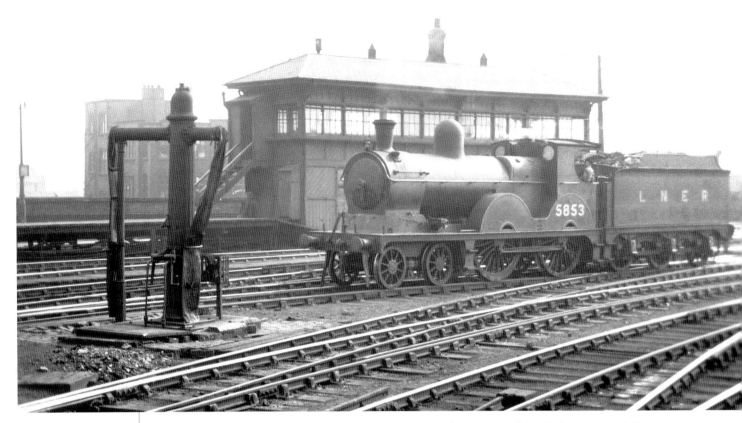

Above: **Central station signal box, 1933.** Following the enlargement of the viaduct approach from two to five tracks, the station was re-signalled. Four boxes were responsible for controlling train movements named, 'A' (quite small, near to the goods depots), 'B' (very large), 'Great Northern' (by the entrance to the warehouse) and 'Viaduct' (above the 'B' route into the station). Standing in-front of 'B' box is D6 class 4-4-0 No 5853 (Gorton, 1898-1946) of Brunswick shed, most probably having hauled one of the trains that made the company slogan, 'Punctual service' between here and Liverpool, possibly this section of the Liverpool to Hull service. Situated at the end of platform 7, the box is adjacent to the water tower and loco servicing area, high above street level, behind it. Note the interesting wood panelling on this hipped roof box. Not long after, the original box on this site was destroyed by an accident and this, larger, 108-lever, replacement opened in 1881. (H.F. Wheeler)

Opposite above: **Arriving train, no date.** Looking across the station throat, this photo captures a rarity on the service from the east coast. The train crew of B17 class 4-6-0 No 2807 *Blinking*, bringing the Harwich to Liverpool boat train into the platforms, will be looking forward to a rest. Another engine will be attached to the rear of the train for its short run to Liverpool Central. On the right is N5 class 0-6-2T performing some shunting. It had a brief allocation to Gorton shed in 1943 and changed its number in 1946. (BPC)

Opposite below: **Central station approach, 1958.** This is the view a signalling engineer would have, facing the station. As can be seen from the extreme left, the whole area is on a viaduct being well above the houses and streets, below. On the left are a pair of lines which curve around to serve the Cheshire Lines goods depot. The wonderful arch of the station's roof dominates the area – and still does. An engine, probably one acting as a station pilot, languishes in the short bay platform, 7, in the middle of the picture. On the right is the new signal box, dating from 1935; sweeping all before it, its 128 levers power operated the points and colour lights. While a leap forward in signalling terms, it was an ugly, grotesque building in architectural terms. The brick cabin was on a concrete floor, hoisted on steel legs set in concrete high enough in the air for trains to pass under it. Just visible to the right of the box is the tender of an engine in the loco. servicing area. (BPC)

Viaduct approach, 1960. Turning around and looking west shows the first mile and a half run outwards from the terminus is exclusively on a viaduct. Arriving, prepared for its subsequent movements, is this train from Nottingham on the down 'B' line. Hughes-Fowler 'Crab' 2-6-0 No 42874 will have arrived by way of Cheadle Heath, Chorlton and the 'A' route at Throstle Nest Junction. A transfer to the other pair of lines will mean that when it continues to Liverpool it will not have to cross over. To achieve this manoeuvre in the station another engine – possibly the one lurking on the left – will have to back onto the coaches which will then set off in reverse direction for the sprint to the other Central station aided by the exit along the viaduct is on a downward gradient. On the right is the girder bridge approach to the GNR warehouse. Above the house can be made out a small engine shed: objections on the grounds of safety from Manchester Corporation meant the company never used it for its intended purpose. (R.K. Blencowe Collection)

Castlefield, 1961. The 1849 MSJ&AR link between Ordsall Lane and Oxford Road was a barrier to the builders of the line into Central station in the mid-1870s. After leaving Central on a viaduct, the line passes over this chord and then drops down at a gradient of 1 in 100 to Cornbrook. Pictures of this solution are rare and so this one, although of poor quality, is included. Dragging its coaches up the final few furlongs to cross above the link lines, almost a hour after it started its journey, is the 7.05am from Buxton with Royal Scot class 4-6-0 No 46158 *The Royal Regiment* in-charge. On the right are the electrified lines of the MSJ&AR, themselves on a viaduct to cross over canals, with its Knott Mill & Deansgate station in front and Cornbrook complex behind us, at which point all tracks will be on approx. the same level. It was in this area that the Joint Line was severed by air-raids in December 1940. (R. Keeley)

Cornbrook

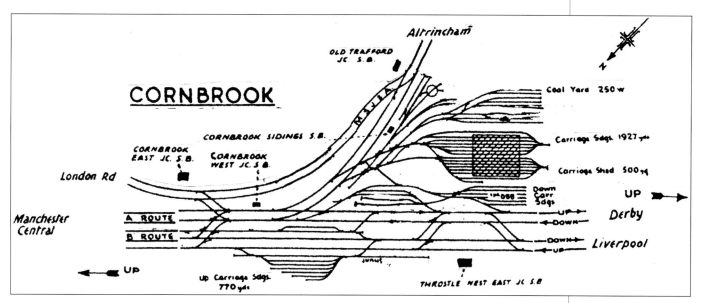

Location Map.

Cornbrook West Junction, 1961. This was taken from a Chorlton-bound train as it passed the wooden signal box. On the right can be made out the supports for the electrified lines of the MSJ&AR. Branching off, immediately to the right of the box, is the link line which allowed trains from Central station access to the line to Chester. Cornbrook West Junction has steadily increased its levers over time, 33 until 1893, 66 until 1907 and then 90. Although not terribly clear, the home signal gantry can be made out. The signalman has pulled lever 80 so raising the top arm while the man in the next box ahead, Throstle Nest East Junction, has raised the lower arm. (Transport Library G. Whitehead Collection)

Above: **Link line, 1951.** A short time after the opening of a station in central Manchester in 1877, Cheshire Lines services switched from along the last parts of the adjacent MSJ&AR towards Oxford Road, to the new station. To achieve a route to Chester, a link was needed between the two sets of lines. This was provided in 1878 when a short, around 250yd, connection was opened between Cornbrook West Junction and Old Trafford Junction. However, possibly due to the need for a longer link to hold trains on, or to ease the gradient, it was extended west the following year. This meant the length was 160yd longer and the gradient eased to 1 in 132 with the junction being almost under Trafford Bank Road bridge. On its way to Chester is a train from Manchester Central, hauled by an unidentified 4-4-0 locomotive. It has just left the quadruple lines from Central and will soon join the electrified MSJ&AR line, on the right. The signal box in the rear is Cornbrook West. Note how tall the down lower quadrant signals are, for visibility, and in contrast to, the squat post for the Joint Line's upper quadrant arms. A bracket signal stand above the second coach, these are for the sidings from the link line. (T. Lewis courtesy Eddie Johnson)

Opposite above: **Cornbrook sidings, 1961.** Although it is tempting to think of signal men as those throwing levers to allow crack express trains to hurtle along, the reality is that most performed more mundane, but necessary tasks. This wooden, small, 33-lever box opened in 1907, controlling the access from the Central station to Chester link line, to a goods and coal yard (capacity 250 wagons) and extensive carriage sidings. As can be imagined, this was quite a busy area with two private sidings (Evans) and there was a loco. servicing area, complete with a 50ft turntable, too so reducing the amount of light engine and train pathways used, to nearby Trafford Park shed. (G. Whitehead)

Opposite below: **Cornbrook Sidings signals, 1961.** This splendid bracket signal is at the entrance to the carriage sidings on the link line towards Old Trafford. There are five home signals. Lever no. 27 in the box was probably the most used as it operated the middle and tallest indicating, movement to the fan of carriage loops. The pair on the left, operated by levers 25 (top) for the goods yard and 26 (bottom), for the locomotive servicing sidings while those on the right (levers nos. 28 and 29) are for the other fan of carriage loops and access to the down sidings respectively. (G.H. Platt)

Cornbrook carriage sidings, 1957. Carriages need to be checked over, washed, cleaned and re-stocked with, for example lavatory paper. When they had been brought here then a small army of staff descended on the coaches. The brick building accommodates their rest room with stove, tables & chairs and washing facilities. In the left background are the remains of the roofless carriage sidings and at ground level are the wooden ramps that enables workers to reach the windows when cleaning them. With factories offering high wages, the railways suffered from a haemorrhaging of its staff, often skilled, to better paid jobs. The national rail strike the previous year was partially about this. Many previously male jobs were now becoming done by women, if the company could get them. (Unknown)

Cornbrook goods yard

Cornbrook goods yard, 1907. Soon after the opening of the link between the Cheshire Lines and the MSJ&AR and a goods yard was accessed from it, opening at the start of 1881. This hand bill was printed and distributed when the new depot opened in 1907. The entrance was on Trafford Bank Road (the home of John Knowles, famous for developing the Theatre Royal in the 1850/60s) from the Chester Road and had facilities for coal merchants, livestock and a goods shed. Adjacent was a building for stabling horses, the main motive power for movement of carts on the streets prior to the early 1920s, although their use persisted well until after the Second World War. (PRO)

Wagon. This five-plank open wagon was built for the company in 1896 by the Gloucester Railway & Carriage Company Ltd. Listed as a high sided goods wagon, it was painted lead colour with white letters and could carry 10 tons. About the time of this wagon's construction, the company owned just over 2,000 vehicles; probably around one hundred would have been cattle wagons. (HMRS)

CHESHIRE LINES

OPENING OF NEW
Goods & Mineral Depôt,
CORNBROOK.

The new Depôt at Cornbrook is now complete, and all kinds of Merchandise can be dealt with in an expeditious manner. A well-equipped Warehouse has been erected, and every convenience provided for dealing with General Goods Traffic, also facilities for dealing with Furniture Vans (lift or on own wheels).

Manchester Traders doing business in the neighbourhood of Cornbrook, Old Trafford, and Salford will do well to make an inspection of the New Depôt (entrance in Chester Road), where full information as to rates, etc., will be furnished by the Agent, Mr. A. J. Hewett.

LIVE STOCK.

The Depôt is within reasonable distance of the Cattle Market, and arrangements have been made for a Special Fast Train to run on Tuesday Afternoons to Knutsford, Northwich, and district.

Further particulars can be obtained on application to the undersigned,

Central Station, Liverpool,
January 1st, 1907.   **JAMES PINION, Manager.**

F/n   J. R. WILLIAMS Co. LIVERPOOL LTD., Printers, 8, School Lane, Liverpool.   No. 58

Cornbrook shed, late 1890s. This three-road shed opened in 1880, complete with a small turntable. The authorisation of the construction of Trafford Park some ten years later illustrates that the growing operational demands were not able to be met by this hemmed in facility, it closed in 1895. MS&LR 2-2-2 engine class 14, No 500, to the design of Sacre, is on the turntable. The canal is very close to our left-hand side. (J. Suter Collection)

Throstle Nest East Junction, 1962. This view is across the running lines, the signal box off to the top left obscured by smoke, with the Bridgewater canal to the rear. The train is the 16.05 from Manchester Central to Sheffield on the 'A' route with B1 4-6-0 No 61011 *Waterbuck* in charge. Between the train and the canal is the 'B' or Liverpool route. The train would have left the terminus as a down train and at this point it becomes an up train. The points between the two routes are for the transfer between them. The complex of pointwork, and the two lower quadrant signals on the wooden post to the right (operated by levers 19, lower, and 20, top, in the signal box) are part of the East Down Sidings. The West Down Sidings are behind us, both parts being used for carriage storage and cleaning. On the extreme right is the distinctive white of Cornbrook West Junction which controls link to the MSJ&AR, which passes behind our position, well off to the right. (C.M. & J.M. Bentley)

Throstle Nest East Junction, 1965. This box is perched in between the four running lines, with the Bridgewater canal behind it. Nearest to the box are the pair of lines to Liverpool, the 'B' route and the box's chief function was to control movement along it, as well as transfer to/from the 'B' route towards Chorlton. The 70 levers in the box also permitted access to the extensive carriage sidings, not only on both sides of the quadruple lines, but between the two routes as well. East Junction was the scene of a fatal accident in 1950, which illustrates the importance of track circuiting. A J11 light engine, from Deansgate goods depot, was Gorton-bound when it was brought to a stop at the junction's home signal on route 'B'. Whilst stationary, a Liverpool bound express ran into the back of the light engine at about 45mph. A 2P 4-4-0 engine and six coaches made up the 7.35am ex-Manchester Central, the light engine was pushed forward about 360yd and the train engine completely derailed. It was judged that the driver of the light engine took too long to follow rule 55 (In clear weather a train must not stand for longer than two minutes before the man goes to the signal box) and alert the signalman of his presence. One passenger and the fireman of the light engine died, and 36 people were injured, three seriously. Track circuits existed from Central station to Cornbrook West junction, the signal box before the accident. (MA King)

West of Cornbrook

Although our route turns south to Chorlton, we are to make a short digression along the CLR towards Liverpool as the engine shed servicing MS&LR engines was a short distance along that route at Old Trafford, as well as the access to Trafford Park sidings and their connections to the Trafford Park Estate and the Ship Canal Railways.

Trafford Park Junction, 1949. Standing on the footbridge over the main lines that leads to the engine shed looking east captures a train that had left Central station a few minutes earlier. Hauling the 5.12pm (almost) all stations train to Liverpool Central is Trafford Park based class D10 4-4-0 No 62651 *Purdon Viccars*. On the right is the signal box. Not only does it control the line off to the left, to the engine shed, Trafford Park Estate and the Ship Canal but also under the bridge in the distance, the curve toward Throstle Nest South Junction. To the rear of the train is an engine in the down loop, probably waiting for the passage of this train before it crosses the main lines to access the line to Trafford Park shed or the goods lines, off to the left. Almost opposite this engine is the single platform for Manchester United fans, with a light engine in the up loop. It may have originated from the shed and could well be waiting for to pass up the main line towards Central station. Next to this engine is a fine bracket signal which controls the main line east but also the curve, ahead, to the right, towards Throstle Nest South Junction. (H.C. Casserley)

Trafford Park Junction, 1960. Pulling its wagons around the curve from Throstle Nest South onto the main down line is O4 class 2-8-0 No 63637 of Gorton shed. The signalman in the adjacent cabin will have pulled lever no. 53 to raise the arm on the right. This will indicate to the driver that his route is into the lines of the Trafford Park Estate or Ship Canal. Old Trafford football ground is in the background with its small wooden cabins that restrict access to the platform used by the shuttle to Central station. (BPC)

Trafford Park Junction, 1970. This is a large, 61-lever, wooden cabin as viewed from a passing train. Notice the company preference of putting the name of the signal box on the front. (M.A. King)

Above: **Trafford Park sidings, 1961.** The footbridge that connected the streets to the engine shed was a wonderful vantage point, the images gleaned as a schoolboy have lasted me a life-time. Beneath us is the down loop, with its link to the down line from Throstle Nest South Junction, as it merges with the down main line looking west. Heading towards Trafford Park Junction along the up main line, is a train of empty mineral wagons hauled by O4 class 2-8-0 No 63701, quite a long way from its home shed at Mexborough. Above the engine are the reception lines (onto which previous picture of No 63637 is most likely destined), and above them are the well-stocked East sidings. At the very end of this long train is Trafford Park sidings signal box. (Bill Hamilton Mike Macdonald Photos)

Opposite above: **Trafford Park station, 1954.** Gliding into the down platform is a train that had left Central station five minutes before, at 12.55pm, Saturdays only. LNER class D11 4-4-0 No 62661 *Gerard Powys Dewhurst* hauls the all stations train, via the Widnes loop, to Hunt's Cross and then Garston before terminating in Liverpool. Serious passengers for Liverpool would have caught a fast train five minutes earlier, the train from Hull taking only 52 minutes. The reason for the inclusion of this picture is to the rear of the train. On the right is the small, 20-lever, signal box. As well as the main line it controls access not only to a gas works on the down side but also an up/down goods loop on the up side, the bracket signal for this is in the distance. By this connection trains from Liverpool can arrive and depart from the sidings. (H.C. Casserley)

Opposite below: **Trafford Park station, no date.** To capitalise on the development of the park, the Cheshire Lines Railway opened a station where, appropriately named, Moss Road was crossed by their line, on 4 January 1904. Heading towards Manchester is a tank engine and six-wheeled coaches. The booking office is in the brick building to the left with a spiral of steps for the Manchester platform, note the station's name painted onto the sides of the overbridge. In the mid-1920s, the suffix '& Stretford' was added to its name. In the background is a tall, 30,000-gallon capacity water tower that the company in the park built. It reputedly cost Metro-Vickers, £1.25m soon after they arrived in 1899. The head of water provided power for the hydraulic lifts and sprinkler system. So that the tower would not be a landmark for enemy aircraft, it was partially dismantled in 1940 and completely removed in the early 1950s. (BPC)

Trafford Park sidings

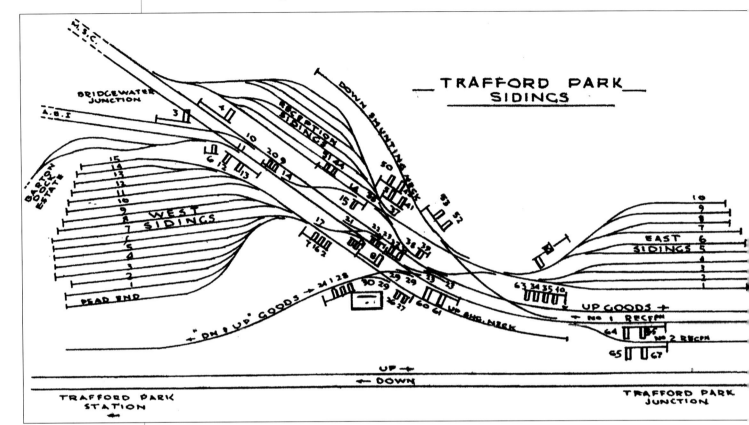

Above: **Trafford Park sidings.** Much of the around one mile between Trafford Park Junction and the next box west, Trafford Park, was progressively developed into a set of sidings to receive and dispatch wagons relating to local industries. These were rail served by Manchester Ship Canal system which in turn, were served by individual railways of the industries of the Trafford Park Estates. (Signalling Record Society)

Opposite above: **Trafford Park sidings, 1984.** Opening in 1904, a box here was replaced by this 65-lever box, probably around late 1920s. Set back from, and with its back to, the main lines, was this brick-built box. It only controlled the East and West sorting sidings, the accesses to the Ship Canal, Barton Estate and industries, but not the main lines. Within its orbit were the bi-directional single line connection to the west, the reception sidings to the east and the up goods line. (J Dixon)

Opposite below: **Long distance freight trains, 1954.** O4 class 2-8-0 No 63599 is typical of the type of engine that would bring freights from afar, for example, arriving at 1.42pm would be the 6.30am mineral departure from Wath, not far from its allocated 'home', Mexborough. At this time, the firms on the Estate alone used 300,000 tons of coal annually. Departures could include for example, 7.00pm to Lincoln or the 9.50pm to Rotherham Road, the engine for the latter would have come light from Gorton, departing at 8.35pm. Near to Mode Wheel lock were the lairages for the cattle market which, being rail connected, sent a TuO 3.15pm train to Sheffield – it is probably seen at Guide Bridge elsewhere. The engine would have come from Gorton at 2pm. In the early 1960s the impact of Mottram yard can be seen in the six pathways from there to here. There were three from Gowhole yard too. Many of the engines seen at the sidings ever called the adjacent engine shed 'home' and while some servicing was done 'next door' much was done at Gorton necessitating expensive light engine movements between the two. (J. Peden)

Local trips trains, 1949. Engines such as an LMS 0-6-0 No 3544 were commonly associated with local trips from other rail sidings like Ashburys, (for example the 1.15am, arriving at 2.42am), Ardwick, Guide Bridge (5.25am departure, arriving at 6.04am) and Dewsnap. Similar engines also performed many stopping passenger turns to Irlam, Glazebrook, Wigan and St Helens. In the background is the stadium for ex-Newton Heath Rovers, aka Manchester United, although the ground is actually in Trafford! Having been bombed on 11 March 1941, the ground wasn't played upon until August 1949 by which time there were trees growing out of the rubble. United played at Manchester City's Maine Road ground for the duration. (H.C. Casserley)

Shunting engine, 1949. With trains to be split up and others to be assembled then humble engines such as N5 class 0-6-2T No 69304 had a role to play. The signalman in the box, just trying to get in on the act to the right, has set the points and the right-hand arm on this wonderful bracket signal with its CLR lower quadrant arms, so that the train enters No 2 reception loop of the sorting sidings. Eleven, including this example, of this class called Trafford Park 'home'. (H.C. Casserley)

The Ship Canal & Trafford Park Estate

While most readers will have knowledge that Manchester Ship Canal had its own railway system, few will know about a similar system to serve the industries of the Trafford Park Estate. This was an island of land north of the Bridgewater Canal and south of the Ship Canal which represented a wonderful place for business to settle and all companies who did establish themselves here were offered a standard gauge rail connection to the Ship Canal railway system, and ultimately, the national complex. Some of the tenants had their own locomotives, many had their railway work done by engines of the Manchester Ship Canal Company. A large volume of traffic passed from the main line railway sidings at Trafford Park, across the Bridgewater Canal to industries in the Trafford Park Estate. In 1931, it was estimated that 3 per cent of the country's total rail tonnage was moved along the lines, which by 1946, had reached 46 miles. The author's mother was one of an estimated 75,000 people employed on the Estate during the Second World War, at 'Metro-Vicks', building bombers. The Ship Canal company had a fleet of tank engines that distributed wagons to the industries. There were two shunts per day by MSC engines.

1955. The desire to rail connect every factory on the Estate meant that sharp curves abounded and so flangeless middle wheels, sliding axle boxes and coupling rods with a 'knuckle' were desirable in the engines that operated the system. The majority of steam engines owned by the Ship Canal company were of the 0-6-0T wheel arrangement. Basically, they were 'Short tankers' or 'Long tankers', 260-gallon water tanks being the difference. One example here is Hudswell Clarke 'Long' tank No 70, dating from 1921, waiting at Irlam with a coach used to ferry workers from Salford. This is an ex-LMS Brake 3rd which cost £220. An over-zealous driver separated the body from the bogies in 1960. With its short, wheel base, 10ft 3in, it could negotiate the sharp curves on the system. Its water tanks held 840 gallons giving it greater adhesion weight and greater operating range. 'Short Tanks' had a slightly longer wheel base and 580-gallon capacity water tanks, it was the latter that was an inhibiting factor when the MSC took control of the lines in the Estate and with the development of Partington steel works and coal basin. (BPC)

1972. Companies setting up on the estate included Proctor & Gamble, Corn Products, Westinghouse, Ford Motor Co. and Kellogg (remember those blue vans sold by Hornby – they had a real prototype!). Several industries employed their own engines for internal movement of wagons. Here a Barclay 0-4-0ST reorganises coal wagons at Corn Products Co. UK works. The extensive nature of the rail system can be gauged by the presence of lines on both sides of Trafford Park Road.
(W.A. Brown)

1948. On the opposite side of Trafford Park Road to the CPC factory was that of Brooke Bond and Thomas Headley (later Procter & Gamble). The latter factory was fed directly from the Ship Canal with its soap based products being distributed through the Estate system. To shunt wagons inside their premises the firm employed a fireless engine as it was cleaner and could be supplied from the factory's water system.
(A. Appleton, courtesy IRS)

1956. The Anglo-American Oil Co. set up in premises on Trafford Wharf Road with a canal-side wharf across the road. Often seen shunting their sidings was this Peckett 0-4-0T of 1897 vintage, named *Alexandria*, but quite when it lost its name and became just No 11 in the MSC Co fleet is unclear. The name plate was on the tanks in the position of the number. Here is No 11, which still retained its previous owner's number, pulling some wagons around the sidings, now as an Esso locomotive having been bought two years earlier, along with the site. (Norman Jones)

1954. Metro-Vickers occupied a very large site in the Park. Amongst other things, they produced Lancaster bombers during the Second World War. Looking over the fence captures some internal shunting being performed by a 0-4-0ST. (A. Appleton, courtesy IRS)

1954. Another large engineering company established early on was that of Redpath Brown & Co. Here is 0-6-0ST in their works. (A. Appleton, courtesy IRS)

British Westinghouse was one of the first large scale inhabitants of the Trafford Park Estate, occupying a prime site in the bend of the Bridgewater Canal. Their factory consumed 11 million bricks, 9 million feet of timber and 17,000 tons of steel. They had three of their own engines (0-4-0ST Manning Wardle). Successive name changes happened via Metro-Vickers and GEC.

'The ideal site for your factory'. This was a brochure promoting the Estate after the First World War. Illustrated are the premises of Taylor Brothers Co. Ltd. on Ashburton Road. From 1907 they started to manufacture railway wheels and axles. With an extensive internal rail system, they had engines of their own which worked inside the factory too. (Courtesy Trafford Local Studies Centre)

RAILWAY WHEEL AND AXLE WORKS OF MESSRS. TAYLOR BROTHERS & CO., LTD.

1949. Taylor Bros. was an engineering firm that made railway wheels and axles. They occupied a large site north of the Bridgewater canal and south of Ashburton Road. Shunting in their extensive internal system is 0-4-0ST No 7. (A. Appleton, courtesy IRS)

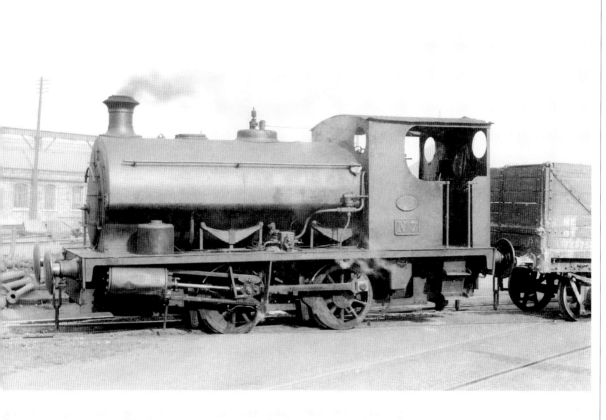

As well as making goods, the Estate expanded into storage. In 1906 a firm, Manchester Warehousing Ltd., was set up to handle the business. By 1915 this amounted to well over 4million cubic feet. As can be seen, many premises were rail connected. This is from their promo. booklet in 1914 (Courtesy Trafford Local Studies Centre.)

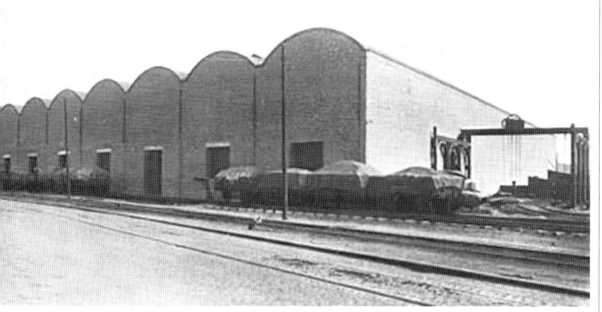

N WAREHOUSE AND 10-TON CRANE GANTRY

Trafford Park engine shed

***Above*: Trafford Park shed, no date.** A shed, replacing that at Cornbrook, was built according to the plaque, opened officially in 1894. There was identical provision for MS&LR engines as well as MR ones. Later, from 1898, the third partner of the CLR, the GNR also was accommodated as their two-road shed at Deansgate was prevented by Manchester Council. Each of the original inhabitants had two, four road sheds. Everything was duplicated. Not only was the accommodation symmetrical, there were two sides to the coaling plant and even two turntables. Note the caps over the smoke vents and the water column. Gorton (September 1900) built ex-GC class 9C 0-6-2T is in L&NER livery although it still has its GCR number, 919. It will become No 5919 from October 1927 and then was rebuilt, in March 1932. Note the '&' in its lettering. (BPC)

***Opposite above*: Trafford Park shed, 1926.** Views inside sheds are rather uncommon. Standing over an inspection pit – as a child it was a challenge to jump across them – is B9 4-6-0 No 6105. The engine was built at the Gorton works of Beyer, Peacock in 1906 as No 1105 and oscillated shed between here and Gorton, mostly. Upon the Grouping it became 6105 and in the 1946 re-numbering became 1469, BR adding a '6' to the front in 1949: this only lasted two months. In contrast to many interior views in later years with crumbling roofs, there is plenty of detail of its construction. Of particular interest, is the trough above the line for the engine's exhaust to be vented off. This led to periodic funnels which opened out through the roof in characteristic chimneys. The acidic nature of the exhaust was the roof's downfall. (H.C. Casserley)

***Opposite below*: Trafford Park shed, 1926.** Not commonly pictured are the arrangements for carrying out repairs to engines. Here, getting attention at its 'home' shed is class D6 4-4-0 No 5856. The engine has been ignominiously hoisted up by its front buffer beam to allow the bogie wheels to be attended to. This simple machine consisted of three steel girders to form a pyramid with a pulley arrangement suspended from its apex. Inside the shed to the right was the winding mechanism: the gearing and the organisation of the pulleys enabled men to lift-up the engine. On the left is an essential part of every engine shed but rarely modelled, a coal stack. Wagon loads of coal would arrive, and the larger pieces used to construct a perimeter wall into which the rest of the wagon would be transferred by wheel barrow. In this way a reserve supply of coal was organised in the event, as in 1926, a miners' strike, so that the railways would have some days' supply of fuel. (H.C. Casserley)

Throstle Nest

Throstle Nest west curve, 1920s. Sometimes a picture of poor quality must be included due to the sheer scarcity of photographic evidence. I know of no other picture of a steam train on this curve. Although many goods trains used this west curve, few passenger trains did. A couple of minutes ago, the signalman at Throstle Nest South Junction had set the points and signals for this train to pass west to Trafford Park Junction. A photographer would have to be quite wide awake as this train (departing Hull at 8.55am) would creep around the curve, obeying the 10mph speed limit. In a few moments it will join the line seen in the top of the pictures, from Manchester to Liverpool Central, at Trafford Pak Junction. No sooner had the smoke cleared from the signalman's view at Throstle Nest South and he would have heard the 'Call attention' bells, from the previous box as hard on our train's heels is the 8.28am from Cleethorpes for Manchester Central. What appears to be an almost duplication of services wasn't quite true as our train was more of an express while the latter stopped at intermediate stations, e. g. Penistone. (H.F. Anderson, BPC)

Opposite above: **Throstle Nest South Junction.** This quite small, 24-lever, box was made necessary by the construction of the curve west from the main line in 1906. This allowed trains from Liverpool and Trafford Park to head south without the necessity of a reversal in the congested approaches to Central station. Looking north from the Chester Road bridge shows the line from Chorlton passing underneath us to Throstle South East Junction. To the left of the signal box is the new addition to Trafford Park Junction. (RCTS Image No B-96-24)

Opposite below: **Old Trafford.** This small section of how this area looked over one hundred years ago is included to illustrate the changing railway scene. The curve at the top is the Ship Canal with the CLR access to the wharfs' access is by a trestle viaduct over the main line to Liverpool and the Bridgewater canal. To enable trains to curve around, as seen previously, necessitated the removal of the viaduct and re-location of its supporting sidings. (Lancashire sheet 104.13. Godfrey Edition, Crown Copyright)

Back on the main line

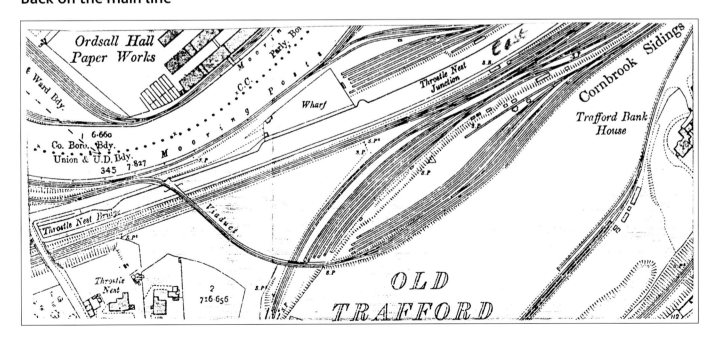

Throstle Nest East Junction, 1959. The sharp curve here serves to keep train speeds low as the approach the junction, from Chorlton. Looking out of the window of a down train shows the end of the carriage sidings on the right. Ahead and this line will join its compatriot from Liverpool on the quadruple approach to Central station. The large bracket signal facing us indicates that we are to pass along the most used route from Chorlton, namely the 'A' route. The other pair of signals would indicate the 'B' route which led to the lower numbered platforms. Above the engine is the junction protected by a similar bracket signal for trains from Liverpool: note that their route preference is opposite to ours. (G. Whitehead)

Opposite: **Leaving Throstle Nest East Junction, 1962**. This Sheffield bound excursion heads south having just left the other pair of lines from Central station as they head west to Liverpool. On the right are the tail ends of the West Down Sidings which together with their opposite cardinal point, and those at Cornbrook, make up extensive carriage accommodation to serve Central station. The tall post next to us contains the home (top) signal for this box and below, the distant arm for the box in-front, Throstle Nest South Junction. BR Standard class 4 4-6-0 No 76089 will enable passengers to enjoy a comparatively cheap and pleasurable outdoor activity, walking in the Peak District, as it will stop at most stations. On the right are a set of steps. The mound they lead to, and where we are standing, once contained sidings that the Cheshire Lines used in 1893 in conjunction with the Manchester Ship Canal, before the connections across the Bridgewater canal and link to Trafford Park Junction were built, in 1904. The wooden trestle bridge mentioned earlier, was probably about where the engine is, across the two pairs of main lines and the canal, descending to a narrow strip of land sandwiched between the Ship Canal and the Bridgewater canal. It connected with the dock lines by Trafford Road. (E. Bentley, courtesy Cathy Marsh)

Above: **Chorlton-cum-Hardy, late 1950s.** Chorlton boasted a reasonably large goods yard on the down side between the Brantingham Road bridge and the station. The loaded coal wagons will probably have been tripped from Trafford Park along the up main line. Using the crossover next to the 24-lever signal box, on the up side, it will have crossed over to the down line. The wagons will have been pushed to a position with the engine under the bridge, directed by the signalman pulling lever No 9 and so operating the just visible small arm, with a 'S' on it, on the post. Now the train, under the capable power of Trafford Park based N15 class 0-6-2T No 69361, is being pulled into the goods yard. The other two lower quadrant CLR signals on the post are, the down starter (upper arm) and the distant for the next block post ahead: Throstle Nest South Junction. Until 1928 there was a signalbox between the two called Seymour Road. (W.A. Brown)

Opposite above: **Chorlton goods yard, 1960.** We are standing on the rising part of Wilbraham Road just before it crosses the line. The station approach is in-front of us with the goods and coal yard beyond the railings. Off on the left is the entrance on the corner with Albany Street. There are several sidings either with mineral wagons or with bagged coal next to them. In the background is a brick goods shed with the signal box to the right. One is struck by the spaciousness of the layout. In-between the pair of sidings is a track wide enough for two horse drawn carts to pass. (Courtesy of Manchester Libraries, Information & Archives, Manchester City Council m188314)

Opposite below: **Chorlton-cum-Hardy station exterior, around 1912.** Just under 1½ miles south of the junction, adjacent to the elevation of Wilbraham Road to cross the line, was the site for the station. This was built by the (MR) and opened on 1 January 1880 having constructed the line from Heaton Mersey, and a junction with the Cheshire Lines, to Throstle Nest Junction, and another junction with the Cheshire Lines system. The buildings are similar to those used on the CLR which is not surprising as the MR was a partner. What lovely carved bargeboard; not sure about the two colours of brick though. While larger stations sprouted cabins to control taxis in later years, they existed many years previously for the same purpose. It looks as if the 'Growler' has a customer. (Lens of Sutton)

CHORLTON - CUM - HARDY. C.L.C.

Above: **Chorlton-cum-Hardy station, around 1912.** Standing on the up platform shows the fancy ironwork used for the footbridge and the two different types of canopies. Worthy of note are the milk churns and under the canopy, a news stand. (Stations UK)

Opposite above: **Chorlton-cum-Hardy, 1959.** Two rapidly moving trains give the impression of trying to shake the station apart. An up-freight train passes through the station, hauled by an unknown engine. The signals it is obeying indicate it will pass onto the MR route at Chorlton Junction, ahead. As a schoolboy, I would sit on the steps, in the background, leading down to the up platform and try to count the number of wagons on freight trains as they thundered through; 60+ wasn't extraordinary. This was quite a busy section of line and so trains such as these had to get a move on if they weren't to mess up the timetable. One of the partners of the Cheshire Lines Railway was the Great Northern Railway who opened a magnificent goods warehouse at Deansgate, adjacent to Central station, over 50 years ago. The company ran four evening express goods trains to Kings Cross and received six morning trains in return, most running passed here. Although by now it was closed to traffic, part of the warehouse was used for parcels traffic while London Road was transformed to Piccadilly, this ceasing in 1970. An unknown K3 class engine heads towards Manchester with an express. (W.A. Brown)

Opposite below: **Chorlton, 1962.** With the platforms of Chorlton station faintly visible under Wilbraham Road bridge, just south, is this signal. The white diamond on the post indicates that the line is on a track circuit and so a light on the track diagram in the signal box will be illuminated. By this simple technique trains couldn't be 'forgotten' and another one admitted to its position causing a crash. It must have been a difficult signal arm to see as a, once white, sighting board has been fitted behind it to make it show up. A few minutes ago, the arm was 'ON' and so the engine, Jubilee class 4-6-0 No 45654 *Hood*, would have stopped. This enabled the couple on the footpath to show their child the spectacle and the footplate crew have joined in the discussions. One wonders if the child developed a life-long interest in railways? The signalman in the box to the rear, Chorlton Junction, will have pulled lever no.16 and if the box in front, Chorlton, has pulled its lever no. 2, then the arm would raise to the position shown allowing the engine to proceed. (M.S. Taylor)

Above: **Chorlton Junction, 1920.** Also meeting at the junction is Manchester South District Railway from Heaton Mersey. This was built to connect the two parts of the Cheshire Lines Railway and was capitalised on by the Midland Railway for its 'Direct Line' to the Peak District and beyond when that opened in 1902. Taken, on a Sunday adjacent to a small, 20 lever, signal box captures the 5pm departure from Central station for St. Pancras along the Midland Railway, hauled by MR 4-4-0 compound No 1031. The lesser used, and so on a shorter post, arm on the right is for the line to Fairfield. (G.M. Shoults)

Opposite above: **Chorlton Junction, 1920.** Heading along the line towards Fairfield is 2-6-4T, its number indistinct, with a mixed freight train. The lower repeater signal arms show up well. Notice the use of tarpaulin to cover goods in open wagons: unless properly tied down these could be a real hazard. (G.M. Shoults)

Opposite below: **Chorlton Junction, 1920.** Emerging from under the bridge and being guided along the Central Station line, is an unidentified, immaculate GCR 4-6-0. On Sundays, the company ran one train to Marylebone serving East Midlands towns. The 'Luncheon Corridor Express' left, appropriately, at 12.25pm and arrived at 5.30pm. Illustrating where the company thought its patronage came from, it was possible to join this train at Fallowfield, 'Stops to take up for London on notice being given at the station'. A later train from London Road departed at 5.35pm was a Restaurant Corridor train arriving at 10.15pm. The latter advertised, 'Dinners served to 1st and 3rd class passengers at the usual tariff'. Passengers really had a choice of routes to the capital to dine on; the L&NWR ran a train from London Road at 4.15pm while the Midland departed from Central at 5.15pm. (BPC)

Above: **Chorlton Junction, no date.** Standing on the road bridge, looking south, gives a good view of the junction. Continuing passed the small MR style signal box is the 'South District' line towards Heaton Mersey and Stockport. Eagle-eyed readers will have noticed that the bridge in the background is much wider than was necessary to accommodate its pair of tracks. This was due to its rebuilding, in the early 1920s; it was made so that any future expansion of the railway system would be able to go ahead without needing to disrupt road traffic. Having travelled rapidly through the southern suburbs of Manchester, the driver of an unidentified B1 will be keeping his speed down to the 20mph through the junction. The tall signal post by the engine will allow unchecked movement of the down Hull to Liverpool express across the junction on its way to Central station. It is leaving MS&LR metals and about to pass onto the CLR joint line. (W.A. Brown)

Opposite above: **Leaving Chorlton Junction, early 1950s.** Keeping an eye on proceedings, the driver of B1 class 4-6-0 No 61161 will soon be able to tackle the short section of up 1 in 340 gradient to Wilbraham Road. The tail end of this express train will be passing through Chorlton station, under Wilbraham Road bridge, shrouded in steam. Guarding the junction is this fine pair of lower quadrant GC signals, and behind them is the MR signal box. (T. Lewis)

Opposite below: **Approaching Wilbraham Road, no date.** Looking west from the road bridge captures an east bound freight coming around the curve having passed through Chorlton Junction a couple of minutes ago. The signalman, in his box at the up end of the up platform some distance ahead, has pulled lever no 21 to lower the signal arm on the tall post to the left, on the 'wrong' side of the track. This, and the adjacent down distant signal, need to be on tall posts to enable them to be seen due to the obscuring nature of the several overbridges: our bridge, Alexandra Road South in this instance. An unidentified LNER 4-6-0 hauls a train of empty coal wagons along the up line over the access to the goods yard seemingly full of coal wagons. To its right are a couple of horse drawn road vehicles and probably a coal merchant's office. (J.M. Bentley)

Approaching Wilbraham Road, 1954. At opening, the leafy suburb sounding name of Alexander Park – well over half a mile away – was used. A name change arrived with a change of ownership at the Grouping, they still were economical as that road was a five minutes' walk away! Stood on Alexandra Road South and looking west captures the line as it turns from south to east: Withington Road bridge is in the distance. About to storm through the station, behind us, is an express on its way to Guide Bridge where this handsome, Gorton based A5 class 4-6-2T No 69823 will be exchanged for a different engine for the trip through the Woodhead tunnel. On the right is the once small goods yard, accessed from our road. Originally a coal yard and siding sufficed but the use of an adjacent redundant airfield for the Royal Agricultural Show in August 1930 saw its enlargement. This consisted of a loop with a wide platform between the lines to allow livestock to be unloaded. (B.K.B. Green)

Wilbraham Road, around 1938. With its warehouse adjacent to Central station, the GNR ran several fitted freight trains from the Midlands to here, daily. J39 class engines were frequently utilised as these powerful engines could put in a good turn of speed as witness No 2693 disturbing the peace just beyond the station. (W. Lees, collection of G.H. Platt & E.M. Johnson)

Wilbraham Road, 1948. A collection of loaded wooden bodied wagons is passing under Alexander Road South as they head westwards. The once haulier of fish trains from Hull and Grimsby, B8 class 4-6-0 No 1353 of Darnall shed passes the small goods yard on the up side. (Unknown)

Above: **Station entrance, late 1950s.** Proudly proclaimed are not only the year of construction (1891), but also the station's original name, (Alexander Park) in atmospherically stained stone above the left-hand entrance to the station. A large and elaborate set of station offices were built where the line went under Alexander Road South, opening on 1 October 1891. Sets of covered steps led down to the platforms. Obviously, the MS&LR expected heavy commuting traffic and so built the stations with pleasing designs, hence the arches over the doors. What a wonderful ornate cupola on the roof. (W.A. Brown)

Opposite above: **Wilbraham Road, no date.** The photographer is facing towards Guide Bridge and we are standing on the down platform. While slightly more than half a mile until Chorlton Junction then the driver of B1 class 4-6-0 No 61161 will now be thinking of slowing down as the engine brings through coaches from Hull. While there are generous, considering the normal stopping train nature of the service here, canopies on both platforms, both were quite a distance from the covered steps from the booking office. As more passengers were expected on this platform, there were more facilities under its canopy. As well as a general waiting room there were toilets for both genders there was a special 1st class waiting room for men. Being less than a fifteen minutes ride into central Manchester the company must have reasoned that a smart suburb would generate a lot of business. While the other stations on this loop line are on a circular route to the centre of the city which meant a longer than a tram ride journey, here and the next station, were well placed for commuting. (W.A. Brown)

Opposite below: **Wilbraham Road station, 1954.** Heading east is the 9.30am empties from Cornbrook sidings to Wath with O4 class 2-8-0 No 63862. It will be keen to make good progress as behind it is an express departure from Central station, the 10.10am to Doncaster. Lever No 20 (out of 23) has been pulled in the small signal box mostly hidden by the tender. If the train needed assistance on the gradient ahead, then the driver would indicate this by giving 1 short whistle when passing here. This would be telephoned to a banker waiting in Fallowfield station, two miles in-front. (B.K.B. Green)

Fallowfield station, 1910. This fine set of station buildings faces onto Wilmslow Road with the line passing at a right angle under it. Above the entrance, on the right, is the name written into the stone with the MS&LR coat of arms above it. A date plate, 1891, is on the left-hand building above the tall window. Ladybarn Road is on the left with the 'Lancashire & Yorkshire Coal Co.' having offices in the station building. Covered ways led down to the two platforms where there were very extensive canopies. From 1 November 1910, the two nearby districts of Withington and Didsbury were added to the title in an attempt to drum up more trade. From 1923 Manchester City Football Club played out of Maine Road and excursion trains of some length would terminate here bringing supporters. Now a pub. (BPC)

Fallowfield, no date. Not only did this line allow passenger trains from Liverpool, and central Manchester, to travel east, but it also enabled the industrial area of Trafford Park as well as the Ship Canal the same opportunities. The signalman has pulled lever no 3 to raise the arm of the up-starter signal. This allows LNER class O4 2-8-0 No 6307 to continue towards Fairfield with a train of empty coal wagons. Over the next two miles to Hyde Road station, up trains faced a stiff climb: significant sections at 1 in 108 or steeper. If the driver had given the appropriate signal when passing Wilbraham Road signal box then a banker, lurking in the down loop, on the left, could, once the train has just passed, be released and by means of a trailing crossover, assist the train up the gradient. Many different classes of engine, fresh from overhaul at Gorton, were sent here for 'running in' purposes. (BPC)

Changing motive power on express trains along the Fallowfield loop

Around 1905. One of Robinson's 'Atlantics' C4 class 4-4-2 No 1083, with its 6ft 9in driving wheels, charges through the station with an up express. Completed by the North British Loco. Co. in 1905 it looks new. On the right is a set of steps down from Ladybarn Road to the up platform. (J. Ryan Collection)

Around late 1950s. Another of Robertson's designs, Pacific A5 class 4-6-2T No 69805. Built at Gorton around the onset of the Great War, it entered service as No 170, becoming No 5170 after the LNER re-numbering scheme. Originally intended to work the Marylebone to Aylesbury service, here they shuttled the Boat Train carriages from Central station to Guide bridge where, from 1954, an electric engine took them to Sheffield Victoria. (BPC)

Levenshulme, L&NWR, 1948. As we journey east, we are passed overhead by the L&NWR, twice. Firstly, by the Styal Loop, the company's answer to a Stockport by-pass then, half a mile later, by the main line to Crewe from London Road. Looking south along the latter shows the quadruple running lines with the bridge over Albert Road at the end of the platforms. The access to this, the Manchester platform, is by a short lane from the main road, along the infamous, 'Road with no Name'. In the distance is a small goods yard, on the up side. If it was the London Road area of the city a passenger wanted, then this line would take you there in a few minutes. However, until 15 September 1952 British Railways had two stations with the name Levenshulme and passengers had to differentiate even after Nationalisation by former company; this became 'North' until 1958. (Stations UK)

Levenshulme station, MS&LR, 1948. Standing on the platform, waiting for a train from Manchester shows the facilities that today would be regarded as palatial and reserved for larger, better patronised station: then it was the norm. The original promoters of the line were onto a loser with this station right from the start, our trains would take just over 20 minutes to reach Central station. Not surprisingly, the service dwindled drastically against L&NWR (and tram) competition. BR named this station 'South' from 5 September 1952 until closure in 1958. (Stations UK)

Opposite above: **Levenshulme station, exterior, 1959.** After passing under the L&NWR main line in a short tunnel followed by Stockport Road, our line opens into Levenshulme station, a mile and a quarter east of Fallowfield. Having its entrance on the main road to Stockport was the MS&LR station in the suburb. The middle door is similar to that at Alexandra Park. The name and date of opening are carved into stone above the right-hand doorway as the gable is larger. Note the wonderfully ornate cupola on the roof. (Courtesy of Manchester Libraries, Information & Archives, Manchester City Council)

Opposite below: **Levenshulme, 1948.** With the gradient, 1 in 100, against the train, the engine is having to work harder to maintain time. B9 class 4-6-0 No 1475 has just passed under Broom Lane bridge, in the background and is passing the suburban goods yard accessed from the lane, the goods shed is about to be obscured by the engine. The line here is in a shallow cutting and the 20 lever signal box is behind us. For most of its life, 1906-49, it was allocated either to Old Trafford or Gorton sheds and, so it was frequently employed on such night-time duties, hence few pictures of them. They were the Deansgate to Ardsley and to Colwick as well as two originating in Ardwick goods sidings, to Lincoln and to Marylebone. (Unknown)

Right: **East of Levenshulme, 1961.** The line curves northwards in its cutting, hence the need for a footbridge to carry a footpath, from the clay pit on the right, to around the United Cattle Products tripe works on the left. The access to the goods yard, over to the left, behind us, passes under the bridge in a brick arch, hence the need for a stop signal for up trains and the point rodding to work the points. This structure is a fine example of how even trifles such as the supporting brickwork were detailed and consequently have a pleasing appearance. Framed by the bridge is Hughes-Fowler 'Crab' 2-6-0 No 42788 just about to pass the signal box on its way to Central station. Having set off from Parkestone Quay at 8am (conveying passengers from the Continent) the coaches will have travelled via March, Spalding, Lincoln and Sheffield. Subsequently, Manchester bound passengers could either change at Guide Bridge (for London Road) or continues as seen here towards Central, arriving at 2.36pm. Just over a hour later and the train would arrive into Liverpool Central, the rather slow last stage due to the reversal necessary in Manchester. (E.M. Johnson)

Above: **East of Levenshulme, early 1950s.** Having just passed over the Sheffield & Midland Joint line from Ashburys to Romiley is a down express with B1 class 4-6-0 No 61154 heading towards Central station, the two-mile marker (from the main line at Fairfield) is on the left. The signalman in the box ahead, had pulled lever no. 20 so raising the distant arm on the post on the right. This is the down signal protecting the access to Levenshulme goods yard. The steel work being erected on the left gives the appearance of a factory under construction. This is the site of a depot for electric engines and EMUs at Reddish. This will be as far west that the overhead electric wires go, the original plan was for them to go all the way to Central station, before economies. Note the '2' post on the lower left. (BPC)

Opposite above: **Hyde Road, entrance, 1959.** The line heads northwards, entering an area of generally poorly drained land where it becomes raised onto an embankment, ostensibly to cross the Stockport branch of the Manchester & Ashton under Lyne canal, but also to pass over the road. Around a mile and three quarters from Levenshulme, where the line crosses Hyde Road – which connected conveniently to Belle Vue – and the company opened a small station. As with the others along the line, the date of opening, 1892 in this case, is carved in the stone above the entrance. Walking through this fine brick arch led passengers into a covered way which connected to the very large station buildings, on the up side. A booking hall, more steps and a subway, would bring passengers to the wooden platforms. The main A57 passed beyond their right-hand ends, the name board is long because it reads 'Hyde Road for Belle Vue'. To the left of the entrance is a notice board, normally advertising trips to the seaside, by rail of course. (Courtesy of Manchester Libraries, Information & Archives, Manchester City Council m27342)

Opposite below: **Hyde Road, pre-Grouping.** A lull in traffic has enabled the station staff to assemble to pose for their picture. Two things stand out from it; they are all male, and their number. Attitudes to employment were very different to today's equality. Prior to the Great War probably less than 5 per cent of the workforce were women. Although this fraction changed a lot during the conflict, due to union insistence, it reverted to a not dissimilar pre-war fraction by 1920. It would take the Second World War and a similar cycle of temporary employment before this mostly male preserve to be broken forever. The number of staff for a small station shows that the railways provided employment for a large number of people. Although not the best paid and with long hours, they were regarded as good employers and steady job. Even the seat has the station had the company carved into the backrest, such was the attention to detail in those days. (J. Ryan Collection)

MANCHESTER, FALLOWFIELD, LEVENSHULME, and GUIDE BRIDGE.—Great Central.

Miles	Up.	Week Days. mrn	mrn	mrn	mrn	non	aft	aft	Saturdays only. aft	aft	aft	Except Saturdays. aft	Except Saturdays. aft	aft	aft		Sundays. aft	aft		
	Manchester (Cen.)..dep.	7 38	8 22	9 25	1125	12 0	12 3	1 8	1 25	3 25	4 28	5 43	6 38	7 20	1030	....	1225	9 0	....	....
3¼	Chorlton-cum-Hardy...	7 45	8 29	....	....	....	1210	1 15	1 32	....	4 35	5 50	6 45	....	....	....	....	....	....	....
4½	Alexandra Park........	7 48	8 32	....	....	....	1213	1 18	1 36	....	4 38	5 53	6 48	....	....	....	....	....	....	....
5¼	Fallowfield..............	7 53	8 36	9 34	....	....	1217	1 22	1 40	....	4 42	5 57	6 52	....	....	....	....	....	....	....
6¾	Levenshulme	7 56	8 40	....	....	....	1221	1 26	1 44	....	4 46	6 1	6 56	....	....	....	....	....	....	....
8¼	Hyde Road.............	8 2	8 46	....	....	....	1227	1 33	1 51	....	4 53	6 8	7 3	....	....	....	....	....	....	....
9½	Fairfield, for Droylsden	8 5	8 50	....	....	....	1230	1 37	1 54	....	4 56	6 11	7 0	....	....	....	....	....	....	....
11¼	Guide Bridge 702..arr.	8 9	8 54	9 45	1144	1217	1234	1 41	2 30	3 44	5 0	6 15	7 52	7 38	1049	....	1242	9 17	....	....

GUIDE BRIDGE, LEVENSHULME, FALLOWFIELD, and MANCHESTER.—Great Central.

Miles	Down.	Week Days. mrn	mrn	mrn	mrn	mrn	aft	Saturdays only. aft	aft	aft	Except Saturdays. aft	Commence 11th inst. aft	Except Saturdays. aft	Except Saturdays. aft	aft	aft	Sundays. aft	aft	
	Guide Bridge........dep.	7 30	....	8 43	9 38	1047	1158	1230	1 50	2 14	5 30	5 58	6 0	6 55	7 29	9 31	4 1	5 17	....
1¼	Fairfield, for Droylsden	7 36	8 11	8 48	....	....	....	1234	1 54	....	5 34		6 4	....	....	....	....	....	....
2½	Hyde Road...............	7 38	8 15	8 52	....	....	....	1237	1 57	....	5 37		6 8	....	....	....	....	....	....
4¼	Levenshulme............	7 44	8 20	8 56	....	....	....	1241	2 1	....	5 41		6 12	7 3	....	....	....	....	....
5¼	Fallowfield..............	7 48	8 25	9 1	....	....	....	1245	2 5	....	5 45		6 16	7 7	....	....	....	....	....
7	Alexandra Park	7 52	8 29	9 5	....	....	....	1249	2 9	....	5 49		6 19	....	....	....	....	....	....
8	Chorlton-cum-Hardy....	7 55	8 32	9 7	....	....	....	1252	2 12	....	5 52		6 22	7 14	....	....	....	....	....
11¼	Manchester (Cen.)..arr.	8 4	8 41	9 15	9 56	11 4	1214	1 0	2 20	2 32	6 0	6 15	6 30	7 23	7 45	9 48	4 17	5 36	....

For OTHER TRAINS between Manchester and Chorlton-cum-Hardy, see page 641; between Manchester and Guide Bridge, see page 703.

1922 timetables. Local services had decreased, due to intensive competition from trams, from the opening frequency of over 20 each way, to 17 just before The Great War. This shrank to 6/7 by The Grouping and in 1953 to just three. Sunday services ceased to exist by 1922.

Hyde Road, late 1940s. A train from Central station has just arrived made up of non-corridor stock, destined for Guide Bridge. The driver in the unidentified class J39 has stopped his train in the best place so that passengers can alight under the canopy should it be raining. While this platform looks in 'as built' condition, the opposite one appears to have been replaced by concrete posts and aggregate infilling, with an oil lamp. Goods provision consisted of a very long siding, here full of wagons: Norman Humphrey was one of the merchants operating from here. Sack loads of coal would be delivered by horse and cart to almost every home. There were two short sidings by the down platform which could have been used for stabling excursion traffic, note the name board. To exit them, drivers whistled to the signal box: 2 long + 1 short whistles for No 1 bay to the up line or 2 long + 2 short for No 2 bay to exit onto the up main line. (W.A. Camwell, The Stephenson Photographic Collection)

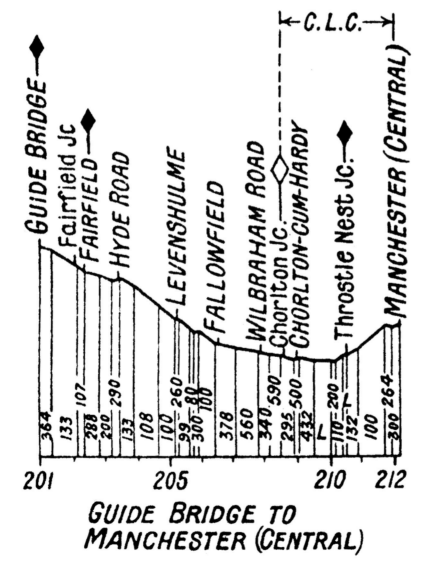

GUIDE BRIDGE TO MANCHESTER (CENTRAL)

Hyde Road, early 1950s. A passenger waiting for a train from Central station would have this view. Two alterations have been performed over the few years between this, and the above, picture. In preparation for overhead wires round to a depot at Reddish, masts have been erected to support them. The canopies, protecting passengers from the rain, have been cut back so as not to foul the OHW. On the gable end of the down platform, the decorative brickwork is visible and steel bodied mineral wagons have taken over wooden wagons in the siding beyond the name board. (BPC)

Gradient profile. This shows the two taking sections of the line, for up trains around Levenshulme and for down trains the approach to Central station.

Poster, 1935.

J 531

CHEAP EVENING EXCURSION

RETURN FARE
1'6
THIRD CLASS

SOUTHPORT

SATURDAY 11th MAY

OUTWARD JOURNEY		RETURN JOURNEY	
	p.m.		p.m.
Ashburys for Belle Vue ....dep.	5 12	Southport (Lord Street) ....dep.	11 0
Gorton and Openshaw .... ,,	5 17		midn't
Hyde Road .... ,,	5 22	Fallowfield ....arr.	12 20
Levenshulme........................ ,,	5 27	Levenshulme........................ ,,	12 25
Fallowfield .... ,,	5 32	Hyde Road .... ,,	12 33
		Gorton and Openshaw .... ,,	12 38
Southport (Lord Street) ....arr.	7 15	Ashburys for Belle Vue .... ,,	12 42

Tickets and bills can be obtained in advance at the Company's Booking Offices and Stations and the usual Agencies

For further information apply to the District Passenger Manager, Manchester ; or the Passenger Manager, Liverpool Street Station, London, E.C.2

THE HOLIDAY HANDBOOK	Price
At L·N·E·R Stations Offices and Agencies	**6d.**

CONDITIONS OF ISSUE OF EXCURSION TICKETS AND OTHER REDUCED FARE TICKETS

Excursion Tickets and Tickets at fares less than the ordinary fares are issued subject to the Notices and Conditions in the Company's current Time Tables

Children under three years of age, Free ; three years and under fourteen, Half-fare

For LUGGAGE ALLOWANCES also see Time Tables

London, April, 1935

━━━ L·N·E·R ━━━

DEAN & CO. Stpt Ltd., Stockport & 41 Moorfields, London, E.C.2—1935—1,250

Above: **Gorton curve, 1954.** Although I've tried to use steam only pictures from before the days of electrification, it hasn't always been possible. This train is a Sunday excursion for Southport. K3 class 2-6-0 No 61966 set off from Ashburys and at Gorton Junction branched off the main lines to appear in this cutting. After Hyde Road Junction, ahead, it will use the Central Station line to travel to Throstle Nest and gain the main line from Central station. After an eastwards trip to Halewood a northerly route along the Liverpool North Extension line and Aintree will be reached. Since the closure of the ex-Cheshire Lines station at Lord Street, trains such as these would move onto the line towards Ormskirk and via the ex-L&Y lines at Burscough, be able to proceed to Chapel Street. (Unknown)

Overleaf above: **Fairfield, around 1900, looking west.** On the right are the pair of original main lines looking towards Gorton with the original Fairfield station being situated about where the road overbridge is in the distance. With the arrival, in 1892, of the line from Central station some six hundred yards east of that original station, it was though best to create a new station to capture passenger traffic from both lines. It would have been possible to have this new line west of the old station. However, the resulting curve would have mitigated against fast running, which the company wanted to promote. Catering for the passengers was a fine brick building on the probably newly created, Booth Road. However, its presence hindered the sighting of down signals hence the elongation of their post so that an express could see it above the buildings. While the up signal at the top of its post is obscured from us, the lower repeater arm is visible. The small, 18-lever, controlling signal box can be seen under the left-hand bridge; there was a small goods yard, opposite it, on the down side. Who says there isn't humour on the railways? An event here, in 1909, could have been tragic, instead it is the stuff for comedy shows. On opposite faces to platforms in the 'V' created are the down fast and the up branch. It was custom to start an early morning train for Central station, not from the down branch but from the up branch. This was because arriving at the down fast platform would have been a train with many parcels for Central station which would need transferring. This was done by the staff trolleying them from one train to another. If the branch train had stopped at its intended platform, the down branch, then this task would have been so much more difficult as the trolleys would have to had been pulled across the tracks on a barrow crossing at the end of the platforms. Having completed their task, the train was given the clear to go at 6.37am and duly set off. However, the signalman hadn't reset the points from the manoeuvre that took the train to that platform and, so it went, not to Hyde Road, but into the goods yard here on the right! Hitting the buffer stop between 6-9mph would have shaken the small number of passengers and caused superficial damage to the train. A signal, interlocked to the points would have avoided this incident. (Author's collection)

Fairfield, 1962. This is the platform that the few stopping trains from Guide Bridge to Central station would have used. In keeping with others along this line, the space under canopies is huge, complete with a lovely arched window for the waiting room. As a through route the line was useful but as a revenue earner for suburban passengers it wasn't. With a journey of 25 minutes to Central station a passenger could have caught a train from other local stations and arrived at London Road, and walked to Central station in less time. The real competition would have been trams and their progeny along the main road to Hyde. (G. Whitehead)

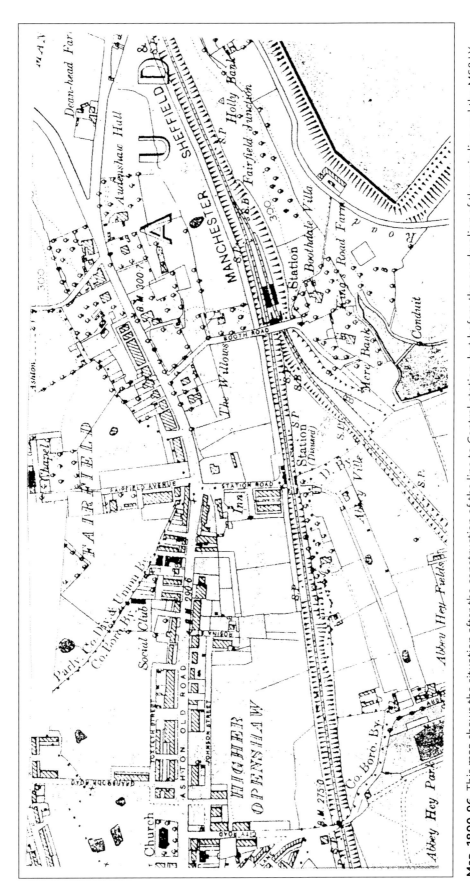

Map, 1890-96. This map shows the situation after the construction of the line to Central station, but before the quadrupling of the main line and the MS&LY changed its name to GCR. To accommodate the line to Central station, the position of Fairfield station had to be moved, from Station Road to Booth Road.
(Crown Copyright)

Above: **Fairfield, for Droylsden, 1951.** In the mile from Hyde Road station the driver has been trying to keep the speed of the engine low as B1 class 4-6-0 No 61250 its winds its way through the curved platforms before joining the main line at the junction ahead; next stop guide Bridge. Signs of change are in evidence on the left. Debris has been created by workmen digging holes for the uprights for the OHW. The vast expanses have an eerie feel about them. A common practise used by railway companies was to have a relief for some of their most popular trains, this was such for the Hull service that left Central at 5.35pm. (Unknown)

Opposite above: **Fairfield, 1950.** Pulling out from the up branch onto the up fast is a train of empty mineral wagons. The driver of O4 class 2-8-0 No 63679 has opened the regulator knowing that he has to get a move on. His train is either destined for Guide Bridge or more likely, after moving onto the up slow line at the crossover just in front of it and judging by the state of the coal stock in the tender, it will head east through the tunnel to Dunford Bridge sidings, or beyond. Controlling the train's progress will be the signalman in the medium sized signal box, 44 levers, just poking above the fifth/sixth wagon. The engine had just spent the last month in Gorton works where its number it had carried for 22 years, 3679, was altered. The new number would last until its demise in fifteen years' time. (N. Fields, Manchester Locomotive Society)

Opposite below: **Guide Bridge, 1949.** This is where the local train service along the line ended. Thus, the noon departure from Central station, on Saturdays only, having stopped at all the six intermediate stations, has arrived at Guide Bridge thirty-seven minutes later. 1899 vintage C12 class 4-4-2T had the 'E' in-front of its number converted into a '6' as can be seen by the number on the side of the coal bunker. It is unclear if the number on the front has had the same treatment. (R. Gee)

ELECTRIFICATION MATTERS

This section relates to the electrification of the line as part of the scheme to energise the lines to Wath and Sheffield. It is not meant to be a complete viewing of every engine, or every mile of the line, more a survey of facets of the railways that were altered due to electrification. The selection has been made along photographed items and upon personal choice; there is no grand plan, just the author's idiosyncrasy.

One of the ideas to surface that would help the country ride out the economic depression of the 1930s, was the 1935/40 New Works Programme. In 1936 the LNER devised a scheme to electrify the line between Penistone to Wath yard via the Worsborough incline, including the section from Manchester to Sheffield, via the Woodhead tunnel. The Glossop branch was included, and the system chosen was 1,500Volts DC, as recommended by the Weir Report.

Trials

Warwick Road, 1941. It was all very well producing a new set of locomotives but before they could be used in public service they need to be tested. Fortunately, the Manchester South Junction and Altrincham Railway had been energised at 1,500Volts DC since 1931 and so was a useful testbed from 22-24 September 1941. One of the tests No 6701 performed entailed involved hauling a train of empty coaches, another 45 loaded wagons and two brake vans and to simulate regenerative braking, two J29 engines were attached and sent in the opposite direction! Note the works plate on the front. Both pantographs are in the 'down' position. (GEC)

Chadwell Heath, 1950. After a few had been built, (in late 1950) they were sent to the recently electrified line from Liverpool Street to Shenfield line. Interestingly, EM1 No 26002 is running with just one pantograph. From June 1951, the lines around Wath had been switched on and the locomotives were sent there for more tests and crew training. (Unknown)

Festival of Britain, 1951. From February to November a display of all that was good and great in the country was put on display. Rationing was still in force and this was an attempt to lift the mood of the country. A crowd of people try to cram into the cab of No 26020. One spin-off from the loan of the locomotive to the Dutch railways was that it was found that the cab was very small and so in production models, it was enlarged, hence the extra side windows. (Rail-Online)

Essential paraphernalia

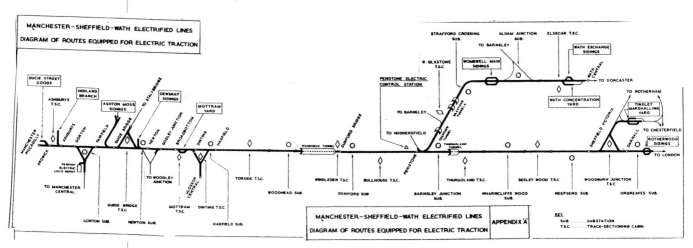

This diagram of the electrified lines shows the extent of the project, the location of sub-stations and where the exchange points were to be. The link to Tinsley yard was a later addition to the plan: the yard wasn't built until the 1960s. (BR)

Aldam substation. With the country still in the grip of austerity and rationing, the fact that BR was building new structures and new technology it was a tonic for all. Taking its current from the local generating board, the line had a series of substations that reduced the voltage and supplied it to the overhead wires at 1,500 volts DC. This equipment was supplied by the North Western Electrical Board, the Yorkshire Electrical Board supling current at Aldam Junction and Neepsend. At the Strafford Crossing and Barnsley Junction substations, special equipment was installed capable of absorbing energy from the regenerative braking on locomotives. (BR)

Penistone control room, 2015. The building is still standing and is used by a public relations firm. (BPC)

Penistone control room, interior, 1950s. A befitting the concept and the era, the control room was very clean and tidy with a map of the entire system on the wall. What a contrast to the dirty image of coal and the continuing post-war austerity. Controllers, in shirts and ties, oversaw the system, adjusting matters using the panel and telephones to speak to other parts of the system. It may look too large for the task entrusted to it: it was as substantially more substations than were used, were provided for. (BR)

New engines and units

***Above*: Doncaster, 1941.** The prototype locomotive, No 6701, was built at Doncaster works during 1940-41 being painted in LNER apple green livery. Following tests at the start of October, the engine was put into store, probably in Gorton. The tests revealed that the engine was quite capable of attaining a similar rate of acceleration as a six-coach suburban unit. It was designed to be operational with just one of the two pantographs raised, however, this proved an unreliable current collector and so both were used. (LNER)

***Opposite above*: Holland 1949.** After several years, both during and after the war, in store, work was found for the engine in Holland after Dutch engineers had discussions with Peppercorn, the CME of the LNER, in England. The reconstruction of their railway system was overhead electric wires at 1,500v DC. Re-numbered 6000, in 1946, the locomotive was sent abroad in September 1947 via Harwich to Zeebrugge ferry. Although seen here with a passenger train at Amsterdam Central on a service to Eindhoven, it wasn't exceptional on such duties as speed wasn't too important then. However, on the comparatively flat lines it was well able to haul freight trains up to 1,750 tons, travelling 400 miles per day, five days a week. During its short stay (five years) it managed to clock up half a million kilometres (200,000 miles). (J.H. Meredith)

***Opposite below*: Return to England, 1956, Reddish.** Upon return to a nationalised network it was repainted black, renumbered 26000 and in recognition of its service to the Dutch State Railways, given plaque and name, *Tommy*. The windows and grilles are different on this side. Windscreen wipers are now in their third position! Given its unique status, it would have been fitting if this locomotive had been taken into the national collection in the NRM. However, for whatever reasons, probably lack of foresight, it wasn't and EM1 No 26020 occupies that position. Indicative of its class, EM1, eventually 57 other locomotives were built in 1950-52. Successfully performing all the tasks needed to run the system both before and after a sister class reigned, one must question the wisdom behind wanting two classes of locomotive and all the expense that entailed. (R.K. Blencowe Negative Archive)

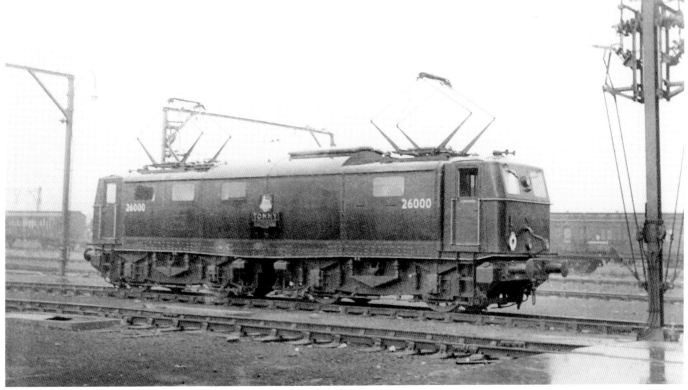

Wath, EM2 class, 1954. It was announced in 1936 that there were to be nine locomotives, of Swiss design, to haul express passenger trains. However, the design adopted in 1949 looked more like a stretched version of the EM1 class: BR ordered 26 such locomotives to be built at Gorton. They would have six motors on two, three axle bogies and were designed for a top speed of 90 mph; rather pointless since the ruling speed along the line was 65 mph. The rationale for so many express engines for such a short line led to the rumour that the electrification was to be extended: in any event it wasn't and the order was reduced to just seven. After construction, the shells were moved down the line to Dukinfield where the electrical gear, from Metropolitan Vickers (in Trafford Park) was added. From new, No 27001, along with two others, were allocated to the new shed here at Wath in black livery, lined with red; the name *Ariadne* would be added in October 1959. One fundamental difference between the two classes of locomotives was the arrangement of their bogies and their underframe. In 1968, the entire class were sold to the Netherlands State Railways. Six were re-built to serve on their lines, ex-27005 was cannibalised for spares. Given their short life and fate, the Presidential Address to the Institute of Locomotive Engineers in September 1953, was more than optimistic when he spoke of the need for more electrification and that the EM1 type engines would be suitable, 'over a wider area'. (Photomatic)

London Road, late 1950s. The driver looks out ahead of EM 2 engine No 27004, which later would receive the name *Juno*, as it waits at the platform's end. It is probably waiting to take a train towards Sheffield, judging by the discs on the front end, denoting an express passenger train. The small group of boys seem suitably impressed by this new type of engine; steam still dominates most of the longer distance trains with diesel multiple units performing local services. The pastime of collecting engine numbers became immensely popular after the war with the Ian Allen book lists selling thousands of copies, even having their own club and outings. However, boys being boys, the presence of the trolley would be too much temptation for some, leading to them being banned from some stations on grounds of safety. The 'London' route of the ex-L&NWR, when electrified at 25kvAC, was very much in the middle of the lines to Altrincham and Sheffield, both at 1,500v dc lines. There were always going to be issues with Ordsall Lane/Ardwick transfer freights passing under two different voltage systems and into a non-electrified area. There was an interesting accident when an EM1 was heading towards Piccadilly with a parcels train. The signalman at Ardwick thought it was destined for ex-Mayfield station, which was a parcels depot, and set the points accordingly. However, the driver of the engine, when he realised that he was being routed from one voltage to the other, couldn't stop the train in time. It could have left the engine picking up AC voltage at one end and DC voltage at the other! However, his quick thinking resulted in the lowering of the pantograph which, apart from electrical problems for the unit, avoided a shut-down of both systems. (S.V. Blencowe)

Safety issues

For 1954 year all electric passenger trains were hauled as far as Penistone, from 14th June, with the complete line to Sheffield starting three months later. However, prior to those dates, trials needed to be completed to ensure that there were no snags that could delay performance. While everything on a plan in an office look fine that doesn't mean to say it is on the ground. For example, electrical continuity and that new locomotives have the necessary clearance and aren't going to take chunks out of platforms! Although not working on electric engines, staff on steam engines needed to take special care too. There have been many instances when the coal has been used immediately next to the hole by the firemen and what remains hasn't fallen in to the space vacated. Consequentially, some firemen have climbed into the tender and using the metal tools, attempted to pull the coal forward. However, the proximity of the OHW has resulted in a tragic accident. Result: explosion; fire; and both power systems failing.

Banking engines, 1923. With the very steep incline up from Worsborough Dale to West Silkstone Junction necessitating the Garrett engine as a banker, it was only natural that thoughts turned to special banking engines when electrification was discussed. The NER had an 18-mile mineral only line near Middlesborough that used 1,500v DC overhead system and had ten locomotives built to run it. Due to the unwillingness to upgrade the overhead system in 1935, the engines became redundant and it is speculated that their use to bank coal trains up from Wath to Dunford Bridge was envisaged. As this would not have fitted into the idea of the New Works Programme (soaking up the large number of unemployed men), this concept remained just an idea. (Photomatic)

New electric units

Fairfield, 1974. To cope with the urban commuters along the line, a series of multiple units were built to operate under the electric wires. The basic three car units consisted of a power car and two trailers, the end one being made so that the unit could be driven from it. These units shuttled between Hadfield, Glossop and Manchester, almost doubling the frequency of operations compared to steam. Most were withdrawn in December 1984 after thirty years' service, having come to the end of their reliable working life. Heading off towards Hadfield, are two three-car units coupled together. Each unit is made up of a motor coach (nearest to us, No M59404), a trailer (M59504) and driving trailer (M59604) which are preserved for posterity at the Bradford Transport Museum. Apart from the unit preserved, all the rest of the 506 class were disposed of at the yard of V. Berry in Leicester. (M.A. King)

Guide Bridge, 1960. This view is included as it shows the 'other end' of the unit, i.e. non-pantograph end as it sets down passengers on platform 3, the up main line. It was possible to couple two three car units, together. They would then provide 348 seats, 300 being second class and so overcoming every commuter's gripe that there aren't enough seats. However, the operator must have a feasible plan of what to do with the other part in between peak periods. Unlike the locomotive counterparts, these units had only a single pantograph located above the luggage compartment of the driving car. When joined together, the pantographs tended to be at the ends of the six-car set. Note how the electric light on platform 3, on the right, has superseded the lone semaphore that sat across above the two lines. (P. Sunderland)

Staff training

Worsborough, 1951. In order to learn the route, new electric locomotives were attached to the front of normal services. It is not clear if the 88tons of the new locomotive are being added to the weight that an unidentified steam engine is having to lift this notorious incline, or if the wires are energised for this short section in order for the new unit, EM1 No 26021, to play its part. It is unclear which, if any, engines were banking the train. (E.R. Morten)

Mottram, 1954. In the original plans, stage 2 was to be the energisation of the lines and branches around Manchester up to Hadfield. However, as events turned out, all the lines west of Dunford Bridge, including through the tunnel were switched on at the same time. For a few months previously, new EM1s were tested and used for driver training between Godley and Crowden. Taken from the road bridge across the complex, an east bound train of empties, hauled by new electric locomotive EM1 No 26019 is chaperoned by O4 class 2-8-0 No 63846. The footplate crew having that rare luxury of allowing their engine to fizzle along while they are hauled up the gradient! At Torside, the train would be switched into the up goods line and at Crowden, come to a halt. The leading unit would be detached and after crossing to the down line, would leisurely go light engine back to Godley. Unfortunately for the crew of the steam engine, they would have to carefully start their train going up at 1 in 117 towards the tunnel. I suspect there were some choice ribald comments between the two crews as they passed each other! (R.K. Blencowe Negative Archive)

London Road, 30 May 1954. Waiting at platform A, ready to take its express train towards Sheffield, is Doncaster based B1 class 4-6-0 No 61159, probably on the Cleethorpes run. A week later and such a train will be under the wing of locomotives such as EM1 No 26008, on the left, at least as far as Penistone. As well as familiarising the crew with how the new machines operate, it was important for the line to be tested to ensure there were sufficient clearances etc. and that chunks of the platform and bridges were not hacked out by the different overhangs between the two forms of motive power. Too tight a clearance was probably the cause of No 26017 'jumping the points' at Tinsley in 1967, not long after the branch to the yard was electrified. (BPC)

Opposite above: **Reddish depot, exterior, northern end, 1981.** The original plan envisaged a single maintenance depot at Reddish, a short distance along the Manchester Central station line from Gorton/ Fairfield between Levenshulme and Hyde Road stations. On the left are two lines into the shed for repairs while the central section had overhead cranes to lift out heavy electrical gear from an engine, below. On the right were staff facilities and stores. As can be seen, in later years, the depot was used for servicing and refuelling diesel engines. Access was from just south of the crossing of the Joint line from Ashburys and was controlled from Hyde Road Junction box, north of Hyde Road station. (M.A. King)

Opposite below: **Reddish, 1976.** While this is an excellent picture of EM1 No 76048, once named, *Hector* and numbered 26048, that isn't the reason why it has been included in this book. To the right is a small cabin, probably used by train crews and other railwaymen. It is of brick construction with metal window frames on the side and front. The rear extension is probably houses toilets. Here the lines south of the depot join leading to a siding, fortunately, there was a footpath the other side of the iron railings. (BPC)

New buildings

Above: **Reddish, interior, 1980**. Engine No 76027(ex-26027) is receiving attention to its bogies by the entire body being hydraulically lifted clear. Opened in May 1954 at 400ft long the shed was built to accommodate EMUs as well as engines. Two three car units could be housed, end on, in the shed. The depot was always more than adequate to handle any repairs leading to the speculation that an extension to the scheme would mean more work here. Some of the EM1 class engines were adapted so that they could work in pairs. (Rail Photoprints)

Opposite above: **Wath, 1958.** Events differed from the initial plan and a smaller depot was also built at Wath, north of the main lines opposite the marshalling yard. It had to have special construction as it was in an area of high subsidence. Both here and Reddish had contact wire in the shed, later, in the latter, it was removed. Waiting its turn outside the shed is EM1 class No 26026 (S.V. Blencowe)

Opposite below: **Darnall depot, 1950s.** Adjacent to the steam shed, a three-road building was planned for the maintenance of electric locomotives. While the concrete inspection bays had lain abandoned since 1940, the structure was eventually completed in 1952. However, although electrified passenger services ceased in 1970, it continued to be used until the closure of the entire electrified system and then was used by diesel engines. The larger depot at Tinsley superseded it. (G. Newall)

New stations

Hattersley, 1980. Although not strictly a consequence of the electrification of the route, more an opportunity resulting from the decrease in trade, I have included them for completeness. The cutting east of Godley was wide enough to accommodate four tracks and so when only two were needed then an opportunity was available for a station to serve the newly expanding housing development here. As can be seen it was achieved by widening the gap between the running lines and constructing an island platform there. A set of steps, and a lift, led to a landing with a ramp to the footpath network. It opened on 8 May 1978. On the left are a pair of class 76 electric engines heading from Mottram towards Godley junction. On the right are another pair of similar engines, Nos 76010/76016 taking coal empties towards the tunnel. (B. Watkins)

Alterations

Hyde Road.

Hyde Road.

Hyde Road Station, around late 1950s. Looking north shows the up platform to be of wooden construction with the signal box at the end. Passenger access would have been up a set of covered steps emerging through the arched opening on the left. On the opposite side of the line was a small goods yard probably to supply local coal merchants There were two bays with platforms, the line next to the down platform, excursion trains need to be parked somewhere, waiting to take passengers home. (BPC)

Hyde Road Station, around late 1950s. The subway opening is much clearer on the down platform with Hyde Road bridge being at the end of the platform. The line here is up at 1 in 80. The station once boasted awnings on both platforms, however, they were cut back before WW2 in readiness for the electrification of the line which at that time, was planned to go right into Central station. Hyde Road station closed to local passenger traffic on 7 July 1958. (BPC)

Other new stations

Stations at each end of the old, dead straight tunnels, could not be used for the new tunnel. A tighter approach curve at Dunford Bridge sliced through the old station there and although on a straight, due to the small curve at the Woodhead end of the straight tunnel, the new station was also sliced through at the western end.

Above: **Dunford Bridge, 1951.** Looking towards the tunnel from the up platform captures a train bursting under the road bridge and into the station. 'Austerity' 2-8-0 No 90255 heads a train of empty coal wagons to Dunford sorting sidings or Wath. To the left can be made out the new temporary road bridge and by necessity, as trains still served the station, the remains of the down platform buildings; the corrugated iron shelter is as good as it gets. Note the access to the platform now that its road link to the Stanhope Arms, off to the left, have been eradicated. In true economical fashion, as parts of the up platform are not in the way they were simply left when the new station was built. (BPC)

Opposite above: **Woodhead, 1965.** We are standing on the new down platform looking back to the tunnels. Built in a similar fashion to the new station at Dunford bridge the bleak and Spartan facilities stand out: befitting the terrain, perhaps. On the left is the water tower and the remains of the old up platform. Its replacement is a simple structure towards the new twin bore tunnel, the platforms are, by necessity, staggered. This, the down platform, couldn't be built more towards the new tunnel due to the river and the up platform couldn't have been built opposite us as there wasn't enough space. Facilities on the up platform were non-existent with a stone shelter sufficing for both platforms. Next to us is the signal box. There wasn't a footbridge. In 1960 there wasn't a real service; up trains consisted of one train (Wednesday, Thursday and Friday only) at 1.11pm and another at 11.13pm, on Saturdays only. The down service was better, one train at 9.38am and another at 11.05, if the guard was given notice. All rather academic as few people used either so closure on 27 July 1964 was no surprise and probably, very little hardship. (BPC)

Opposite below: **Mottram, 1967.** On the main line, adjacent to the 'Hump' signal box and the staff offices at Mottram yard, a pair of platforms were built, date uncertain. As men signed on in Gorton and their charges were here then they could easily catch one of the regular electric trains that plied the route. The halt only appeared in the working timetable. (Stations UK)

The new Woodhead tunnel

Building the tunnel, 1950. While the conditions that the workmen endured during the building of the first two tunnels a century earlier were truly horrific, great efforts were made that such state of affairs was not repeated. After authorisation for a new tunnel on 15 November 1948, a 'mini' town was built almost above the Dunford bridge end of the existing tunnel. This was to cater for the over 1,100 workmen and would be needed for well over three years. In the goods yard of Dunford Bridge, a series of wooden huts were erected for stores and other needs. The land directly in front of us has been cleared and whilst the down platform at the station is still there, their buildings have been removed to make way for the new lines. With associated repair workshops, office and engineering staff as well as the location, several miles from the nearest towns, and the bleakness of the climate, then supporting them became a mammoth task in its own right. It is early days yet when O4 class 2-8-0 No 63631 passes through the station on the up line with another train of empty coal wagons, almost oblivious to the contractors' offices, to the right. A small town springing up, above where the new tunnel was being built, consisting of 48 wooden dormitory huts, cinema, dry/wet canteens, shop and post office and first aid facilities. On 26 October 1953 all was auctioned off, save the sewage works, especially built to be of use to the village when life returned to normal. (BWLB Brooksbank, Initial Photographic)

Opposite above: **Section of new tunnel.** This differs from the two other tunnels as the summit is some way inside the tunnel as opposed to being adjacent to the Dunford Bridge portal. Whereas the old tunnels needed several ventilation shafts, this has only one, nearly midway, a 16ft diameter shaft, 467ft deep. An old shaft (No 5) was also connected into. In modern times, this lack of ventilation has been cited as an Achilles' heel for re-using the tunnel with diesel trains as there would be inadequate airing of diesel fumes. The summit of the line is almost half way along the tunnel. From the Dunford Bridge end the line rises at 1 in 1,186 from the east and at 1 in 129 from the west. With Manchester Corporation extracting so much water from the River Etherow, it was important that any water flowing from the tunnel workings did not contaminate this and so a special purification system was built. (BR)

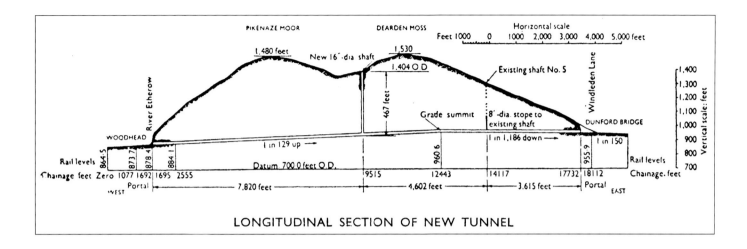

LONGITUDINAL SECTION OF NEW TUNNEL

The new tunnel

Woodhead end, 1953. Having emerged from the down tunnel, K2 class 2-6-0 No 61852 will head towards Godley. Even at this late stage, the overhead mast for the up line is still in place even though it will never be used. This was a curious feature of the plans to use the tunnels for the new electric line. One of the reasons why a new tunnel had to be built was, as announced on 15 November 1948, 'restricted profile (of the old tunnels) prohibiting the erection of overhead wires...' Over optimism or bad planning when in 1936 the LNER authorised electrification using the existing tunnels? A crane sits on the new bridge built over the River Etherow. The single new portal is receiving its dressing of stone. B.W.L.B. Brooksbank Initial Photographics)

Tunnels, 1950.
Tunnels are often built by driving a smaller, 'pilot', boring followed by the full-scale tunnel, later. Such tunnels were driven from each portal and central vertical shaft. Although the original tunnels had several shafts to help produce a smoke clearing draught, there was no need for more than a pressure equalisation outlet in the new tunnel from which steam engines were banned. Steel bracing was used, and the tunnel was concrete lined. (BR)

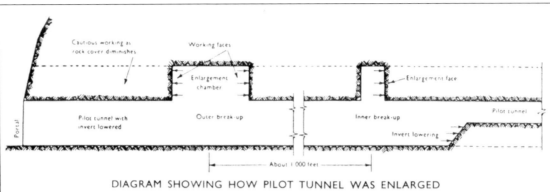

DIAGRAM SHOWING HOW PILOT TUNNEL WAS ENLARGED

ENLARGEMENT OF PILOT TUNNEL NEAR DUNFORD BRIDGE PORTAL

Miners meeting, 1951. Boring was started in February 1949 with this momentous occasion happening on 16 May 1951. Mining was not all plain sailing as new rock formations and water, previously unknown, are encountered. One section near the Woodhead end collapsed in June 1951, taking six months to clear. Special recesses were constructed to allow for the overhead wires to be attached. (BR)

View inside new tunnel. In contrast to the old tunnels which were straight, this new one curves at a radius of 40 chains (880yd) to allow easy connections at the Woodhead end. The tunnel was steel lined, finished off by using cement. Two shuttering machines were built and ran on a special track. When in position dry concrete was brought in using a narrow-gauge line, mixed and pumped between the shuttering and the rock. The white appearance of the tunnel stems from the permanently lit bulbs and that the material has not been sullied by smoke as steam engines are not allowed to haul trains on their own through the tunnel. (BR)

Dunford Bridge end, 1954. Like its predecessor, the entrance to the tunnel at this end was in a cutting. The old tunnels are to the right. (BPC)

Woodhead portal, 1954. The line at the western end emerges right out from the rock face and an ornamental portal was built. To the left are the two old tunnels which will have metal grills over them. Their subsequent use for electricity cables so as to preserve the views on the hills led to coolants being used resulting in steam arising from the old ventilation shafts. A notice next to the portal would read 'No 71 Woodhead tunnel 5340yards'. (BPC)

Woodhead opening, 1954. Although completed by October 1953, after some 4 ½ years construction and at a cost of £4.25m, it was not officially opened until the June of the next year. At the Woodhead end, a trailing point was inserted into the old down main line and so locomotives etc. could use the new up line for training and civic purposes. A train load of dignitaries witnessed one of the new electric locomotives, EM1 class No 26020, break a white tape stretched across the tunnel mouth with the Minister at the engine's controls. Afterwards he traversed the tunnel and alighted at Dunford Bridge and, in true railway tradition, the party retired to a hotel for a celebratory lunch-in Sheffield! The locomotive currently resides in the National Railway Museum at York. (BPC)

Commemorative plaque. This was originally fixed to the left-hand side of the portal at Woodhead. After the line's closure, to protect it from theft, the plaque was removed and is now close to the ticket barriers on platform one at Manchester Piccadilly station. The day after opening of the new tunnel, freight trains from Wath continued to Mottram rather than the previous exchange over point at Dunford Bridge. Electric passenger trains linked Manchester with Penistone from 13 June, but passenger services didn't start going all the way to Sheffield until 14 September 1954. (BPC)

Gorton, 1951.
Although the frame, bogies and body were constructed at Gorton, the electrical interiors, built by Metro-Vicks in Trafford Park, were installed at the carriage and wagon works at Dukinfield, a short distance east along the main line. Ignominious as it seems, the shells of the engines were towed between the two sites just like an ordinary mineral wagon. Believed to be EM1 No 26020 is the train behind a dirty and impossible to identify the 2-8-0 engine, complete with brake van. (J. Fairclough)

Old buildings, early 1950s. There were two bridges over the line west of Brookfold signal box, along the line from Godley junction to Woodley. One was enlarged with a new stone arch accommodating the longer up loop. The other was simply blown up. (BR)

Old uses for New buildings, 1953. To accommodate the steam engines that plied their business between Manchester and Glossop/Hadfield, a single-track shed was built at Dinting. As can be seen, it offered the minimum of facilities, namely water and coal. A steam engine waits outside the other end of this brick building of unknown construction date. After the EM1 class locomotives were built in 1950/1, they were surplus to requirements until 1952 when many congregated at Wath as well as hauling trains up to Dunford Bridge, the remainder were built in that year. Some of the sidings here had wires built over them and some engines were stored here. Hopefully the workmen on the side of the engine is cleaning the sides and will not attempt to get on the roof! This was later home to the 'Bahamas Society' where they stored the Jubilee class engine. (L&GRP)

1st day: switch on!

When the 'juice' was switched on, officially, between Wath and Dunford Bridge on 4 February 1952, then loaded coal trains could be taken up the notorious Worsborough incline as far as the eastern end of the Woodhead tunnel, at Dunford Bridge. Often forgotten, this really was the primary objective of the scheme.

Penistone, first day. Arriving along the down main line into Penistone at an otherwise unheard-of speed is EM1 class No 26012.

***Opposite below*: Wath, February.** A loaded coal, on the left, prepares to leave Wath yard. Its pantograph, and that of its banking locomotive fellow EM1 class No 26041, on the front right, have their pantographs almost to the maximum, 18ft. The exit from the yard at Elsecar Junction is across a road and at level crossings this was the rule. (H.C. Sanderson)

Penistone, 1st day.
The lead locomotive was followed a short while later by the banking locomotive, No 26017, as the train heads for Dunford Bridge. The control centre is in the building to the right. (G. Newall)

Penistone, 1st day. Heading for Barnsley Junction are a pair of EM1 class engines, Nos 26025, leading with 26017 to the rear. They will take a train of empty coal wagons down the Worsborough incline. The extra locomotive will not only weight wise, act as a brake, but also the pull of gravity on the wagons will enable its motors to act as a generator, putting energy back into the wires. (G. Newall)

Exchanges at Dunford Bridge, February 1952-June 1954

Down trains

Dunford Bridge, 1953. Having got the train to the top of the incline, the electric locomotive needed to be exchanged for a steam engine for its onward passage through the tunnel and down towards Godley Junction. Of course, to achieve this substitution, the train needs to be stationary and so a banking engine will be 'buffered up' not only to give the train an initial start, but also to push it over the summit of the line, just this side of the tunnel mouth. Over fifty years old, J11 class 0-6-0 No 64289 is restraining the train from going backwards, down towards Penistone, awaiting its slot through the tunnel. The down sidings were used as a waiting area for steam engines waiting their opportunity, they were laid level so that any train backed up into them would, upon releasing the wagons brakes, would not have the steep gradient that the main lines are on, to contend with. (B.W.L.B. Brooksbank)

Dunford Bridge, 1952. Banking the rear of a train of wooden, some private owners' wagons, is EM1 class No 26020, providing not only weight, but also power to prevent run-aways. (Rail-Online)

Dunford Bridge 1953. This is the view out from a passing passenger train. O4 class 2-8-0 No 63598, having been swapped for an electric locomotive, waits in the down loop. While the passenger train's exhaust is clearing in the tunnel, the O4 engine will, by an exchange of whistler with the banking engine, head west. (Mile Post 92½ Picture Library AWV Mace Collection)

Up trains

Dunford Bridge, 1953. The up sidings at Dunford Bridge were the main collection and sorting area for empty wagons returning from Lancashire via the tunnel. Very long up/down loops were controlled by two signal boxes, No 1 on the up platform and No 2 where the loop joined the up main line, some half a mile distant. No 2 box also controlled the access, from the up loop, to four loops, around 400yds long. These coalesce to the left of the 55ft turntable, seen here from a passing down train, onto which an unidentified 2-6-0 is travelling. Note the parachute water tank and the single storey mess building for drivers, guards and shunters. Beyond are sixteen loops, around 300yds long, controlled by No 3 box, into which the empties are sorted so that they can be sent back to their originating colliery smoothly. No 4 box oversees the uniting of the loops and is next to the plume of smoke in the distance. Beyond is space for coal to be stacked, in case of emergencies and two long, 300yd, loops lead onto the down main line by No5 box. (Mile Post 92½ Picture Library AWV Mace Collection)

Towards Sheffield, early 1950s.
Of-course, not all wagons originated from Wath and so some had to be sent down the main line to Sheffield to collieries east of the city. With its lamps indicating its brakes are connected to those of the engine, is O4 class 2-8-0 No 63707, heading down the obvious gradient. (G.W. Sharpe)

All change, almost

London Road, Saturday 12 June 1954. This is probably one of the last steam hauled service along the ex-GCR route to the capital that could be photographed, the 3.55pm. At least passengers, if they could afford it, had a restaurant car for enjoyment during the 5 hours 25 minutes journey. Services from the other side of the station, using the ex-L&NWR route would take ninety minutes, or less, to achieve the same. It may seem that the engine, K3 class 2-6-0 No 61828, is a light-weight for such a task, but given the 5 or 6 coach load, it should have little problems keeping to the timetable. (Rail-on line)

Above: **Stalybridge, Sunday, 13 June 1954.** All traffic was suspended from using the old tunnels while the engineers occupied the lines. They severed the old lines and connected the main lines to those that entered the new tunnel. At around 9am the next morning and the 08.30 Manchester London Road to Marylebone express, electrically hauled, breezed past and into the new tunnel. During the changeover, trains that normally used the tunnel were diverted and, with a reversal at Huddersfield, could regain their former metals into Sheffield Victoria. Here is probably the 10.25am from London Road to Marylebone. At Guide Bridge, K3 class 2-6-0 No 61910 will have used the original SA &MR line to Stalybridge. Using the middle lines there, it will avoid the platforms and head off ironically, to the Standedge tunnel through the Pennines, to Huddersfield. (Unknown)

Opposite above: **Wath exchange sidings**. While most railway enthusiasts are familiar with the marshalling yard here and some will know of the shed built here to accommodate the electric locomotives, few are aware of the loops built, probably at the time of the shed's construction, around 1951. Separated from the yard by the quadruple running lines, these loops were principally for trains that did not need sorting in the yard and only needed to exchange their motive power. The Wath West curve, built by the MS&LR in 1882 enabled trains from pits along the S&K to access Wath yard. Trains from further afield along the S&K, destined for cities in the west, could use the Woodhead route by this curve, but after electrification, would need to exchange engines. The two northern loops were used by up trains, that is electrically hauled from the west. Upon arrival in a loop, the electric locomotive would be uncoupled and would move off, depending upon its next task. A steam engine would back down from the turntable are in the south, couple up to the wagons and then set off east. In the opposite direction, down steam trains would arrive into one of the two loops nearest the main lines. After uncoupling, the steam engine would, again depending upon its next task, move off. It may go to either one of the head-shunts in-front of it or traverse the complex and access the turntable area. A water column was also available. Meanwhile, an electric locomotive would reverse from one of the head-shunts to be coupled onto the waiting wagons. The train would then set off west, through the Woodhead tunnel and so into Lancashire/Cheshire. With most of its work done during the hours of darkness, it has been almost impossible to obtain photographic evidence. (GCRS)

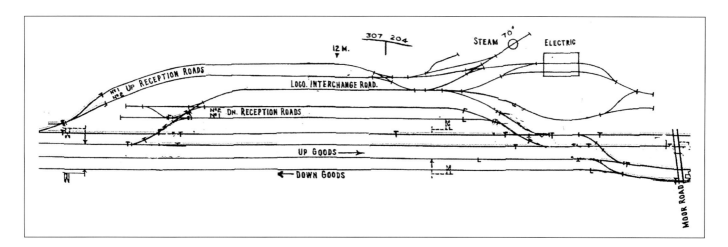

Wath, 1953. Waiting in the loops are several EM1 class locomotives, namely, 26011 and 26039 note the OHW for the marshalling yard in the background. Although initially a protestor about the new S&K line when it was proposed, the GCR actually used it more than its joint owners. Some down freight trains using the line, heading for York in 1961 were: 9.10pm from Trafford Park, 7.30pm from Huskisson and 5.10pm and 9.45pm from Dewsnap. A selection of up freight trains from York were: 8am and 9.45pm to Mottram. (both M.H. Walshaw)

Exchanges at Penistone, June to September 1954

With the current switched on between Dunford Bridge and Penistone (and down to Wath) from February 1952 and between London Road, through the tunnel to Dunford Bridge in June, it left the section from Sheffield still needing steam haulage.

Up trains

Above: **August.** J39 class 0-6-0 No 64824 is ready to depart with a train from Manchester. It may appear odd to have such an engine hauling an express train but the real issue for trains was the mostly, 1 in 120 down gradient and preventing the coaches over powering the braking capacity of the engine and coaches. The EM1 locomotive that brought the coaches through the Woodhead tunnel is in the left background, awaiting its return task. (E.R. Morten)

Opposite above: **September.** The 9.54am express from London Road departed behind the EM1 locomotive almost hidden on the left. Upon arrival at Penistone, the electric unit will have uncoupled and crossed over to the down main line. B1 class 4-6-0 No 61114 will have been waiting, possibly on the down line, and when the pathway was clear, would have crossed over to couple up to the waiting coaches. After releasing their brakes, the train will depart for Sheffield, a just over twenty minutes journey. (LCGB, Ken Nunn Collection)

Down trains

June. What a busy railway scene! Penistone station is actually cut into the side of the slope and the grassy mound on the southern side was a great place to watch trains from. Local interest is maintained by C13 class 4-4-2T No 67424 in platform 1, probably waiting to take its coaches to Doncaster or Sheffield Victoria, it being a Darnall engine at that time. Looking as if it is departing for Barnsley is an unidentified J11 in the background. The real attention is for the train arriving from Sheffield behind a B1 engine. Pulling into platform 2, it will ensure the coaches' brakes are on before being uncoupled to be replaced by an electric locomotive. (BPC)

September. The 9.30am from Hull Paragon has been dragged up the gradient from Sheffield and 'parked' in platform 2. The hauling engine is in the distance and will probably avail itself of the 50ft turntable on the down side in readiness of a return trip to Sheffield. Meanwhile, EM1 class No 26011 has emerged and is backing down to couple onto the coaches. If this seems a lot of effort, at its Guide Bridge stop, the process will be reversed so that a steam train can haul the coaches to Manchester Central. There, another steam train will be attached at what was the rear of the train to haul it to Liverpool Central. (Rail-online)

Exchanges at Sheffield Victoria

Up trains

These would arrive across the Wicker Arch and mostly go into platform 4, the up main. The electric locomotive would be uncoupled from its coaches and then it would move forward then set back with a destination being a short siding off platform 2 to await its return trip. Meanwhile, often waiting in the Middle Siding was a steam engine which would move forward then set back onto the coaches. After coupling up and a brake test it could continue east. Four to five minutes was allowed for this manoeuvre.

1966. Two locomotives are being exchanged. An unidentified electric engine has brought a train into platform 4, has uncoupled and now languishes in the middle road. Meanwhile, under the watchful eye of a worker (notice no high vision jacket in those days), B1 class 4-6-0 No 61360 waits. Soon it will attach itself onto the rear of the coach and deposit east. Being a Doncaster based engine, its destination may well be Hull. (S.V.B Lancove)

1956. EM2 No 27000 *Electra* has been uncoupled from its coaches and is heading along the platform line. A workman is preparing to climb out from the track-bed onto the platform. He will have to guide the steam engine slowly until it contacts the coaches and then get back down to couple the two together and the brake connection – a very hazardous task. Waiting to take over is a B1 engine in the Middle Siding. (R.K. Blencowe Negative Archive)

1960s. Odd as it might have seemed in the new electric era, but there were through steam workings at Victoria station. The South Yorkshireman express linked Bradford, Halifax and Penistone with London and exchanged steam engines here. Waiting in the Middle Siding to take the train south is B1 4-6-0 No 61201 while Class Five 4-6-0 No 44695 awaits relief: passengers will be jostling for seats totally oblivious to the exchange that is about to happen unless the driver of the B1 engine is a little too heavy on the power when reversing! (N.E. Preedy)

Down trains

Steam hauled trains for Manchester would arrive from the east and, usually pass onto the down loop which serves platform 2. As they do so, they will pass their replacement electric locomotive languishing in the dock siding. After uncoupling, the steam engine would pull forward and then set back into the Middle Siding to await its pathway, depending on its task. The electric unit would pull forward passed the signal box and then set back onto its coaches. Ahead is the route across the Wicker.

1950s. Arriving with an express from the east is D11 class 4-4-0 No 62670 *Marne*. EM2 No 27002, which will be named Aurora waits, ready with its Manchester head-code. (R.K. Blencowe Negative Archive)

1958. Still un-named (later *Pandora*), EM2 No 27006 waits adjacent to the Royal Victoria Hotel. (R.K. Blencowe Negative Archive)

Victoria station, 1956. With a new electric railway in its midst, BR took the logical step to improve the appearance of Victoria station as well. This included a new booking hall and inquiry office, new toilets, a refurbished waiting room as well as a lick of paint! Alterations were also made to the external appearance, to accommodate rails sworn enemy, cars, as this view up the approach road shows. The war memorial was moved within the booking hall. (BR)

Exchanges at Guide Bridge

Following the abandonment of the plan to run the electric wires around to Manchester Central station, then trains from the east destined for Central station – mostly the Boat Trains – had to have their motive power changed at Guide bridge, in both directions.

Down trains

1960. Arriving into the down fast line is the Boat Train from Harwich at 1.43pm. EM2 loco. No 27003 *Minerva* has electrically hauled it the just over 36 miles from Sheffield Victoria. After uncoupling it will leave the coaches with no engine. (Peter Sunderland)

Late 1950s. While engines from Trafford Park shed were frequently seen on such sprints to/from Central station, they were no means exclusively used. I wonder what is going through the mind of a member of the footplate crew of A5 class 4-6-2T No 69817 (from Gorton shed after 1954) as he watches an unidentified electric engine that has just come off his train that he now awaits to depart. (A.G. Newall)

1960. Having been lurking just beyond the platform end on the branch at Stockport Junction, Stanier 2-6-4T No 42472 has emerged and backed down to the coaches. With the time rapidly approaching 2.09pm it will be time for it to depart for the short trip (11¼ miles, 20 minutes) to Central station. There another engine will be attached to the end of the train, this engine detached and the train departing for Liverpool. (Peter Sunderland)

Up trains, 1960

When electrification came to Guide Bridge, one alteration performed was to build a short bay, not for coaches or vans, but for locomotives, into the island (platforms 3/2) at the up end. Arriving at the up main platform is the 2.10pm from London Road to Sheffield Victoria, hauled by EM2 class No 27000 *Electra*. The end to end journey would take 56 minutes.

Shortly afterwards, a steam hauled passenger train arrives from the east with Stanier 2-6-4T No 42560 in-charge.

After stopping and uncoupling, the steam engine will have moved away, and the electric engine we saw earlier will emerge from its bay and attach itself to the front of the coaches. Class EM2 No 27006 *Pandora* will depart at 2.43pm to take the Boat Train as far as Sheffield (arriving at 3.24pm) where the reverse operation will be performed. In pre-electric days e.g. 1949, then there would be no need for the Guide Bridge exchange. The equivalent train, 2.15pm from Central, would arrive into Sheffield Victoria at 3.31pm, after a non-stop journey. (All, Peter Sunderland)

Exchanges at Godley Junction

Godley, 1968. Loops alongside the CLR platform here were used to exchange motive power. Arriving from Yorkshire is a train of loaded coal wagons behind EM1 class No E26055 *Prometheus* and is proceeding along the through siding. Meanwhile, sister engine No E26021 creeps by the disused up platform with a train of similar steel bodied wagons, now empty, ready for return to Wath. Trying to hide in the background is the controlling signal box: Brookfold. It housed 41 levers and lasted until 1981 when vandals set it on fire. (Both Peter Hutchinson)

Godley, 1964. In preparation for the exchanges here, the loop alongside the up line towards Woodley was extended, westwards. So, an east bound train of empties would pull into the loop, detach the engine, which light engine, would make itself ready for the return trip. Here, Stanier 2-8-0 No 48261, probably having brought the wagons in the rear, is heading west. Many trains were banked all the way from Stockport Tiviot Dale station to Woodley or beyond, to here. (C.M. & J.M. Bentley)

Godley, 1968. Prior to the arrival of a steam hauled train from the west, an electric locomotive, E26021, has crossed from the down side to the up loop and has moved forward into the small siding at the end. Then, arriving behind Stanier 2-8-0 No 48322 was a train of empty wagons. After detaching from them, the steam engine is moving forward and will pass onto the up side to avail itself of the turntable. Afterwards, the electric locomotive will reverse and attach itself to the train in the up loop. Maybe the second locomotive will attach itself to the front and the double headed train will set off for Wath. (Martin Welch)

Opposite: **Godley Junction, 1964.** While the electric locomotives could be driven from either end, the same could not, generally, be true of steam engines. Consequently, trains arriving from the west would need to avail themselves of the 70ft turntable for the return trip. Contrary to popular views, other engines hauled the coal; trains other than 2-8-0s. Here, Class Five 4-6-0 No 45282 is being stabled at the turntable after turning in readiness for the trip west. (John Fairclough)

Ashton Moss

Exchange sidings

Crowthorn Junction, 1960. A short piece of track connects the L&Y and GC main lines in Ashton under Lyne: it is part of the OA&GBR, a joint MS&LR and L&NWR venture. In-front of us is the MS&LR line to Stockport Junction, at the western end of Guide Bridge station, while behind, are the exchange sidings next to the L&Y line. Off to the right is a L&NWR branch to Denton Junction. By this latter route, Guide Bridge, and a reversal, could be avoided, enabling direct Oldham to Stockport running. Pictures of trains on this stretch of line are extremely rare and so this one, despite its poor quality, is included. Arriving from Guide Bridge is a freight train under the control of EM1 No 26036 passing under Birch Street bridge. At South Junction, ahead, it will veer off left towards North Junction signal box. This will allow a shunting engine to remove the wagons and to sort them into the sidings. (Neil Frazer)

Ashton Moss South Junction, 1963. After the lines north emerge from under Richmond Road, the sidings fan out with access being controlled from this large, 70-lever, brick Great Central signal box. The OHW didn't encompass the main lines, the one before the box being a reception line for the eastern group of sidings, behind the box. The signal post to the left with two shorter arms controlling movement from them. Ahead on the main line would be the ex-L&Y line at OA&GB Junction. (G. Whitehead)

Ohps! Ashton Moss, 1964. Even though the OHW went some distance west of North signal box, hiding on the left, the siding/head-shunt wasn't of infinite length. Falling foul of this is EM1 engine No 26052. The wagons it was hauling have been removed, its pantographs have been lowered and presumably, the 'juice' switched off. Now come the tricky job for the breakdown team, probably from Gorton, to pull the engine back onto the track. With the underframe/bogies and body being separate it will need care and expertise to achieve re-railing. The depot's crane is at the end of the tools vehicles. Adjacent to this line was Ashton Cricket Club and when a steam engine, often an O4 class, waited in this siding, if the wind was in the wrong direction then its exhaust meant sometimes a case of, 'smoke stops play'. (G. Whitehead)

Locomotive exchange at Ashton Moss

Above: **Steam, 1956.** Standing on Richmond Street bridge, looking across the triangle of lines towards OA&GB Junction, gives a glimpse of the extent of electrification here. On the right is the 'main line' from South Junction to OA&GB Junction, with wires over the loops next to the line. Sorting out empty wagons is a Standard class No 75075, they await collection by an electric engine for transfer to Dewsnap sidings for further sorting. Curving away in front of us to the left, are the electrified lines completing the triangle to North Junction. Usually, loaded wagons were brought around along this line by electric engines, and then forwarded by steam engines. (M Roughley)

Opposite below: **Ashton Moss Sidings, 1955.** Looking east towards Ashton under Lyne shows the L&Y line between us and the houses, and a fraction of the West Curve across the bottom right. Lines in the triangle were organised into two groups. Those to the east, alongside the Guide Bridge to Ashton line, were mostly loops while those in the northern section, seen here, were mostly blind ending. EMI Class No 26042 shunts the sidings here before returning to the mainline at Guide Bride. Being an 'island' of electrified lines in a sea of other lines sometimes meant that engines were exchanged for comparatively short journeys which was not only time consuming, but expensive. (K. Field/RAS)

Electric, 1963. We are standing just south of Richmond Road bridge with South Junction box trying to make an appearance under it. The driver of EM1 engine No 26015 is looking out of his cab window at events further back; the two lines nearest us continue curving around to meet the ex-L&Y line at North Junction. (G. Whitehead)

Rotherwood sidings

Coal, from the Derbyshire/Nottinghamshire coalfield, joined the MS&LR to the east of Sheffield at Worksop. Also arriving on the lines east of Victoria station was coal from the collieries locally, north and east of the city. Their route to Lancashire was through Victoria station and up to Penistone. However, when electrification was planned, there needed to be a change-over place so that electric could replace steam traction. A sight, east of the city, near to Darnall shed, adjacent to the line south from Barnsley/Mexborough and Orgreave colliery, was selected. A series of up and down loops were built, probably sometime during the Second World War, with access points being Rotherwood, in the east and Orgreave Colliery in the west, and energised on 3 January 1955.

Rotherwood, 1977. The brick cabin housed a 46-lever frame. Its construction was so that it could withstand all but a direct hit from enemy bombs; it was most likely commissioned in 1942. The running lines are in-front of us with a with a large stone slab protecting the middle of this otherwise glazed cabin. As well as controlling movements along a short section of the quadruple main line, it controlled the exit from the five up loops and the entry to the four down loops. At the ends of the up loops was a trailing access onto the main lines in readiness for return workings, or for access to Darnall shed. The overhead wires ended about 550yd beyond the exit of the loops on the up side. Steam hauled coal trains from mines to the east would pass into the down loops and an electric locomotive would take over the haulage over the Pennines. Darnall steam shed was a short distance along the line from the ends of the loops for the servicing of the steam engine. (John Hinson)

Rotherwood, 1961. Loaded coal wagons and empties were moved to the pit heads by steam engines. Here, an unidentified O4 class 2-8-0 organises mostly steel bodies mineral wagons. A water column and a 70ft turntable were also provided, on the up side. (R.A. Savill)

Orgreave Colliery, no date. This box controlled the eastern end of the exchange loops as well as the branch to the colliery, top left. The driver of K3 2-6-0 No 61824 is keeping a close eye on the road ahead as his train passes the 60-lever box on the run into Victoria station. Note the coke wagons in the background: there was a coking plant adjacent to the colliery. (S. & A. Warnes)

***Above*: Orgreave, 1977.** With yet a different style/capacity, a coal train emerges from the down loops onto the main line as it heads towards Victoria station. Now, the 20T capacity wagons, variety HAA are in a rake of 20 on the merry-go-round principle, probably for Fiddler's Ferry power station near Warrington. To haul such loads, two EM1 units were coupled together and driven from the leader, No 76012 with 76027 behind, emerging from the western end of the loops. (M.L. Boakes)

***Opposite above*: Woodburn Junction, 1960s.** Heading west towards Victoria station with larger capacity wagons is EM1 class No 26055 *Prometheus*. To ensure the locomotive can fit under the footbridge, its pantographs are retracted almost as far as possible. Off to the left is the line north towards Tinsley: later it will be energised too. Note the single line above the wagons, this leads up and across all the running lines to the engine shed at Darnell. (G.W. Sharpe)

***Opposite below*: Victoria station, 1958.** A train of wagons on the down goods line passes No 4 signal box as it by-passes the platforms, much to the amazement of the boy in short trousers, under the watchful-eye of his mother. Having alighted from the departing train from platform 4, he probably nagged his mother to have a look at this new-fangled locomotive. EM1 No 26014 is waiting for a suitable pathway for it to cross over onto the up main line to reach its line, up the incline towards Penistone. (S. Paul collection S. Needham)

Above: **Victoria station, 1963.** Meanwhile, heading in the opposite direction, coming off the Wicker arch is an east bound train of steel bodied empties, bound for Rotherwood. The driver of EM1 No 26045 casually surveys the scene. Although some track-work alterations were performed at the other end of the station in December 1948, work at this end of the station went ahead in 1953. No 3 signal box, which was to the right of the wagons on the up side, was replaced by a 60 lever box just to our left, just at the start of the arch, on the down side. (M.L. Boakes)

Opposite above: **Dewsnap sidings, 1954.** Now redundant from its prime job of banking trains out of Wath sorting sidings in Yorkshire due to the electrification of the lines: two electric engines doing the work of four steam engines, and ascending the bank quicker. The question is, what role could this engine perform? Slow moving coal trains caused congestion and so fewer, longer trains were an answer. To haul such trains needed increased motive power; double heading meant two train crew's wages. Consequently, the possibility of larger engines was looked at. One experiment performed was to use this massive engine, Garrett 2-8 8-2 No 69999, built by the LNER in 1925. To investigate fuel economy the engine was converted at Gorton, to burn oil, here it is waiting to depart from the sorting sidings towards Woodhead. Whatever the results of the trials with this engine, no more was heard of it nor the idea. With a balance of payments problem and indifferent results the trials were not pursued. It does seem rather antiquated to put coal into small wagons that can carry no more than ten tons and to make up trains of 60 or so of such wagons. Larger wagons were available, but most pit heads were unable to accept them, and the owners were unwilling expensively to alter their sidings/loading arrangements to suit the railway companies. To give some idea of the amount of coal mined in the UK in 1913, the figure was 287 million tons of which 73 million tons were exported. In 1993, that was the total amount mined in the UK. The engine eventually went to Bromsgrove to assist trains up the MR line. This wasn't a great success and so it was withdrawn from service. (B.K.B. Green)

Other exchange places

Ashburys, 1960s. Transfer freight between the 'other' part of Manchester's railways (the Victoria/Exchange routes) at least to Ordsall Lane could not be entirely electrically hauled. Shunting in Ashburys' yard is Gorton based J11 'Pom-Pom' 0-6-0 No 64437, probably having arrived from Miles Platting or performing shunting here. (Rail-online)

Dukinfield Central, 1959. Arriving from Guide Bridge is one of the small number of passenger trains along the line, trams and buses having drained most of their traffic away. The Peak Forest canal passes under the station, approximately under where we are standing on bridge No 3. Overhead wires are only over the up line with this extending right through the station, over the bridge across the River Tame (again) and over Cavendish/King Street bridge, being anchored on the eastern side of the road bridge. However, the limit for electric engines, with some margin for 'human error', was above Lower Alma Street, just before the river is crossed. This enabled electric engine to arrive from the Sheffield direction and for the end to be clear of the point work at Dukinfield Junction. The whole train could be divided and shunted into the Avenue sidings by the electric engine. While fine in theory and planning, it is doubtful if this manoeuvre was practised often, and then at night, hence the lack of photographic evidence. (Stations UK)

Midland Junction, 1965. Carefully bringing train 1Z13 from the MR's Ancoats branch onto the L&Y's Ardwick branch is Class Five 4-6-0 No 45073. Originating in Stockport, probably Tiviot Dale station, this train will have threaded its way onto the MS&LR at Ashburys. At West Junction, it would pass onto the Ancoats branch, skirt around the MR goods depot, pass over Ashton Old Road and come to lie alongside the Ardwick branch, albeit, at a different level. The two branches join and then pass over a subway and under a footbridge connection the homes on Midland Street (on the left/right?) to the David Lewis play-ground, on the left. Ahead and the train will join the L&Y Ashton branch, and after Miles Platting station descend the incline there to access the line to Southport. This area was always seen as a place for the exchange of engines between the MS&LR and the L&Y. On 4 April 1929, a train from Hull to Blackpool had come to a halt for such a purpose. A light engine struck the coaches in the rear, shaking many passengers and injuring the guard, who later died. The OHW stopped a short distance north of here. This idea was that this enabled long electrically hauled trains to occupy this line and for shunting engines to remove parts and feed them into Ancoats goods depot. A crossover just behind us, under the footbridge, would allow an engine to be released to perform other duties. By the same process, in reverse, trains could be assembled from wagons withdrawn from Ancoats depot and then electrically hauled away. I have been unable to discover any photographic or oral evidence that electric engines actually used this line. However, being freight-dominated, and these activities happening often at night, they may have occurred and no one recorded them. During the re-building of London Road station, express trains enacted a similar procedure from January to April 1960. This time it was electric engines that brought their trains along the branch to here. They were exchanged for steam engines for the trip to Victoria. (Eric Bentley, courtesy Cathy Marsh)

Hyde Road, 1955. Following the abandonment of the plan to energise the Central Station line, at least as far as Old Trafford, then a site to exchange types of motive power was needed. Here, on the down side, are two coal sidings, one very long (almost 300yds) in use by a local coal merchant and a pair of shorter sidings either side of a platform. They became used for engines, one steam and one electric, both accessed from the up and down lines. Electrically hauled freight trains for Trafford Park from Guide Bridge would come to a halt next to the signal on the down line. After uncoupling, the engine would pull forward and access the siding, as seen here EM1 engine No 26002, the siding having OHW for the purpose. From the other siding another engine, steam, would emerge, couple up to the front of the train and off it would go west. In the up direction, trains would come to a halt next to the stop signal by the signal box. Then a (steam) engine would be exchanged for an electric engine which could set off under the wires, easterly. (G. Whitehead)

Steam workings

To 'feed' the electrified lines, steam workings were necessary.

London Road approaches, 1955. Carrying the multiple track approaches to the terminus is a very wide viaduct, more a long series of arches really. Not only does this carry the two company's parallel lines but also the extra tracks produced to serve the goods warehouses. About to enter a platform line, probably with a train from Sheffield, is EM2 No 27006 Pandora. No matter how sleek and fine the express service is, there is still a need for the coaches to be removed to a servicing point, allowing the engine to be released. Performing this humble, but necessary role is LNER C14 class 4-4-2T No 67451. It will take the coaches to the carriage sidings next to Ardwick goods depot. The engine will also bring fresh carriages into the station for the express engine to take to Sheffield. (G. Whitehead)

Aldam Junction, 1965. With its rear coal wagons passing the junction and its signal box, 'Austerity' 2-8-0 No 90633 heads towards Wath on up goods, probably returning empty wagons to the yard. The bracket signals almost hidden by the paraphernalia for the electric locomotives is for the junction: left had arm for the branch up to Wombwell main and the right-hand arm for the line to New Oaks and onto Barnsley. For most of its life it was allocated to Wakefield and with the L&Y connection at Barnsley Exchange to the GCR then it may well have come from that direction. (Les Nixon)

Penistone, no date.
An unidentified
EM1 class electric
locomotive pulls
into platform 2,
down main, after
dragging its coaches
up from Sheffield
Victoria. Meanwhile,
seemingly like a relic
from another age,
an 'Austerity' 2-8-0
heads onto the up
main with a working
from Huddersfield. Its
subsequent route will
be under the wires,
possibly empties to
Wath yard down the
Worsborough incline,
or down to Sheffield.
(BPC)

Worsbor' incline

Above and opposite above: **West Silkstone Junction, no date**. The standard format for coal trains
supplying the power station near Warrington was for their high capacity wagons to be pulled by a pair of
EM1 locomotives, here Nos 76032 and 76034, while at the rear, another pair of EM1 locomotives, here
76026 and 76027 (note the different positions of the grilles and windows), push the train. At the top of the
incline, the rear pair will come off and when a suitable pathway occurs, go back down to Wombwell sidings
to repeat their task-very similar to that performed by the unique Garrett steam engine. (Both Rail-online)

West Silkstone Junction, 1979. Having arrived at the junction, the up train, hauled by the furthest EM1 locomotive, will come to a halt. Attaching itself to the front is EM1 class 76040. The whole train will now descend the notorious Worsborough incline, with much at 1 in 40. Not only does the leading unit provide a weight that the load has to push against but also its motors can be used as generators: this regenerative braking enables current to be put back into the system as well as acting as another set of brakes. (Rail-online)

Wombwell exchange sidings

Wombwell Main Junction, no date. After leaving the main line at Aldam Junction, electric trains climb at 1 in 75 for just over half a mile to reach Wombwell Main Junction. Branching off left from it is the connection to Wombwell colliery: the controlling signal box is out of the window on the other side of this train. Ahead can be seen the line curving to the middle right, behind the bracket signal towards Woodburn Junction and Sheffield Victoria; the 1 in 63 gradient must be a challenge. On the extreme right can be seen a forest of gantries and wires. Sometime during the 1940s, three loops were built on both sides of the lines as it curves around the tight curve to Swaithe Junction and then into Worsboro' Dale, the gradient of down at 1 in 202 being very noticeable. With the connection from New Oak Junction arriving here, on the right, it was reasoned that steam hauled coal trains would arrive at this point and a facility to change to electric traction was necessary. Our train is being signalled along the main line between the loops, which loop a train would be directed into would be shown by the short arm and an electric number indicator, 1, 2 or 3. A mass of rods and wires passing from under our line go to the controlling signal just to the right. The exchange loops here allowed trains from the Barnsley and Stairfoot areas to change their engines to electric traction before continuing their journey west, without the necessity of taking their train to Wath yard. (Railway Correspondence & Travel Society G-228-16A)

Wombwell, 1981. A lot of activity is going on in the up side of the loops. Nearest to us are EM1 class locomotives Nos 76006/024 have been given the pathway down the line towards Wath yard. Next to them, awaiting their next task, is another close coupled pair, Nos 76028/27 while on the left is No 76051 in the head shunt at the end of the up loops. Note the massive steel structures necessary to support the overhead contact wires. (Rail-online)

Wombwell, 1981. Engines that could work in pairs are recognisable by the all yellow front end as well as there being two jumper connections. Between 1968 and 1970, a set of 21 engines were adapted to operate 'merry-go-round' air braked coal wagons. This had the advantage of allowing longer trains and so the limited number of pathways could be used better Setting off from the loops is a loaded train heading for Lewden crossing and up to Penistone, literally, at a gentle, 1 in 415, initially. EM1 locomotives Nos 76006/24 will most probably have another pair of locomotives at the rear which will come off at West Silkstone Junction, the time taken would be about half that of steam hauled trains. (Rail-online)

Tinsley yard

As part of the modernisation plan, many small goods yards and sorting sidings in the Sheffield area were amalgamated into one large marshalling yard, between two parts of the former MR system, connected by a piece of former GC line: The Sheffield District Railway. Passing through the area is the Woodburn to Aldam Junction line, also of the GCR. Spurs were built, both up and down, connecting the SDR to the

Arrival, 1979. This train of empty wagons, hauled by EM1 class No 76035, from either Sheffield or Rotherwood directions, has passed up the line through both Attercliffe and Broughton Lane stations (closed) to enter the yard. It is passing to one side of a small, two road, shed and will soon enter the reception lines. Above is the control tower with one of the three unique to here, 'Master & Slave' units used to push a train load of wagons over the hump. Basically, these were two 08 diesel shunters permanently coupled together with only one cab. They would push an entire train over the hump where the wagons would be 'cut' depending on their destination, and gravity would pull them down into the correct sorting siding, aided by special braking systems. (Railphotoprints.uk Collection)

line from Woodburn. The line from Woodburn Junction, north through the sites of Attercliffe and Broughton Lane stations, to Tinsley marshalling yard was electrified in 1965. Where the line passes over the former Sheffield District line at Catcliffe, two spurs were built connecting the SDR and the former GC line, the southern chord was energised. This allowed trains to arrive and depart from both north and south on to the GC system from the western end of the yard. Similar spurs at the eastern end of the yard allowed access to the ex-MR system. It is interesting that only a dozen years after the main line was energised at 1,500 volts DC, the insulators used here were capable of being used at 6.25kV AC if required with the option of 25kV AC with minimal conversion costs. Unlike similar electrified marshalling yards, to save on costs the main body of the sorting sidings was not electrified: only half of the arrival sidings was electrified for incoming electric trains; Departing electric trains either had to use the southern third of the main sorting sidings (the western part of which were wired for electric trains) or had to be drawn out of the main sorting sidings by diesel locomotives into electrified departure roads where the electric locomotives were attached.

Reception lines, 1980. As can be seen, the construction of the yard entailed the removal of a vast amount of soil and rock to create the flat conditions necessary for hump shunting. A few of the loops have had wires constructed above them to allow electric trains to enter them. (M.A. King)

Mishaps

Trains and gradients are seldom good bed-fellows and so many mishaps happened.

Thurstone, no date. Unguarded level crossings are a problem that is still prevalent today. I hope the occupant(s) of this small car could get out in-time. It probably stalled/became stuck as they tried to cross the line, some 150yds in the background. The wreckage has been moved onto the down loop. (Transport Treasury)

Opposite: **Closure of services, 1981.** With the view that passenger services were restricting freight pathways over the line, the passenger trains and stations along the electrified lines were closed: Stockport and the Hope Valley was the route now between Manchester and Sheffield. Only the Manchester suburban service from Hadfield and Glossop was retained. On 10 March 1981, the 07.30 Warrington to Tinsley train hauled by class 76 Nos 028 and 029 derailed in Dinting station. Here the aftermath is being cleared up during the four-day closure. Thereafter, the up line was not restored being singled between here and Hadfield. A reversal of a train conveying tankers across the Pennines derailed a short while later, causing a full-scale emergency. Due to the cost of repair and changes to business, it was decided to close the electrified line. (J.F. Ward, J. Suter Collection)

Final straw

ACKNOWLEDGEMENTS

A single book, let alone a series, is probably impossible to do on one's own so these volumes only exist due to the efforts of many people, organisations and public bodies. First and foremost, must be the support and help from John Scott-Morgan and the rest of the editorial team at Pen & Sword. Bob Gellatly of the Great Central Society as well as the Signalling Recording Society and the Industrial Railway Society have been a wonderful source of information and knowledgeable people who have all given their time and expertise freely. My thanks go to Richard Casserley for sorting through his father's collection. The local studies sections of several libraries have been a mine of information namely: Tameside, Stockport and City of Manchester and their archives contain many useful pictures. Jon Harrison's IT support has been invaluable. Mention must also be made of Joe Lloyd, John Dixon, Mike Addison, Graham Whitehead, Brian Wainwright, Geoff Alsop, Graham Hague, Mike King and Jeremy Suter. Individual people have been attributed by photographs; my apologies if I've omitted anyone. In this digital hi-tech world pictures can be cloned and sold in many markets, often without the taker's agreement. If I have bought and used one of your pictures without your knowledge, then please let me know.

End piece

Newton, no date. Although the gradient is against the train, at 1 in 185, it will not be taxing the engine too much. A3 Pacific No 4474 *Victor Wild* makes a stirring sight as its shatters the peace of Newton and prepares to roar through the station on its way towards Woodhead. On the right are not only two private owners coal wagons but part of the extensive goods yard, complete with a large, 25T crane. (E. Oldham)

BIBLIOGRAPHY

A starting point for any book about the MS&LR must be the excellent trilogy by George Dow, first published in 1959, a veritable mine of facts, data and views. Over the intervening years there have been many books about parts of the system, chiefly, the 'Woodhead' section which have provided a perspective on matters by Kenneth Oldham, Jackson & Russell, Stephen Batty, Eddie Johnson's trilogy and Alan Whitehouse. A huge number of books, periodicals, plans, timetables and ephemera have been consulted in the preparation of this book, principally:

- *Great Central* volumes 1-3, George Dow.
- *Regional History of GB*, volume 7, The West Midland, Rex Christian.
- *Wartime Woodhead*, Eric Oldham.
- *Profile of the class 76s & 77s* by David Maxey.
- *Railway Passenger stations* by Michael Quick.
- *BR layout plans* vol. 13 by John Swift. (Signalling Record Society)
- The Godfrey Edition of 25 inch to the mile maps.
- *Cheshire Lines Committee Signal Box Register* by Mike Addison & John Dixon.
- *Signal Box Register Volume 3 (LNER)* by the Signalling Record Society And apologies for those I have omitted.

Other volumes in this Great Central Railway Series include:

- Mainline operations Sheffield.
- Joint lines around Manchester & South Yorkshire.
- Mainline operations Lincolnshire.
- Mainline operations East Midlands including the LD&ECR.
- Joint Lines to Marylebone.
- Joint line partners in the Cheshire Lines Railway.

INDEX

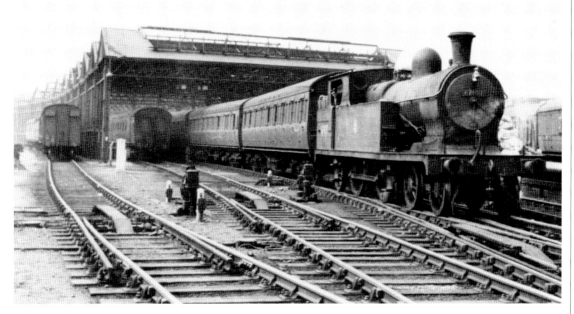

Mayfield, 1954. To the west of London Road is the 'overspill' station at Mayfield. Opening on 10 August 1910, its originally three, later four, platforms were connected to the main London Road station by a large tall, long, covered footbridge over Fairfield Street; what a nuisance this was. Useful as it was it probably only became indispensable when London Road was being transformed into Piccadilly in the later 1950s. A stopping train for Hayfield waits to depart, and in doing so will execute the manoeuvre that trains today do from platforms 12/13 which want to proceed east; it will have to cut across all the exit tracks from the parent station stopping all inwards and exiting movements. The author well remembers arriving on the 'Pines Express' from Gloucester – standing room only – into Mayfield in the late 1950s. Although this book is about the GCR side of London Road, this photograph shows a GC engine on a GC service from this L&NWR extension. (BKB Green)